THE ROAD TO WIGAN PIER

Books by George Orwell

GEORGE ORWELL

THE ROAD TO WIGAN PIER

WITH A FOREWORD BY VICTOR GOLLANCZ

A HARVEST BOOK • HARCOURT, INC.

ORLANDO AUSTIN NEW YORK SAN DIEGO LONDON

PUBLISHER'S NOTE

The Road to Wigan Pier was first published in England in 1937. It was commissioned by the Left Book Club, which flourished in the thirties. The aim of the club, according to one of its brochures, which reflects the temper of the time, was "to help in the terribly urgent struggle *for* World Peace & a better social & economic order & *against* Fascism, by giving (to all who are determined to play their part in this struggle) such *knowledge* as will immensely increase their efficiency." Members of the club received each month a book selected by a board of editors made up of Victor Gollancz, Harold Laski, and John Strachey. The book selected was issued in a special format and sold to members at the low price of two shillings sixpence. In 1937 the club claimed more than 38,000 members.

The board of editors asked George Orwell to write a documentary report on conditions among the unemployed in the north of England. He carried out this assignment, though he wrote about people who were still working as well as about the unemployed. In the latter part of the book, however, he went on to discuss, from his own Socialist but highly individual point of view, what he considered to be wrong with Socialism and Socialists.

Orwell delivered the manuscript to Victor Gollancz

and then went to Spain to observe and take part in the civil war, which was then in its second year.

The Road to Wigan Pier was duly published by Victor Gollancz, Inc., under the auspices of the Left Book Club, with a foreword by Mr. Gollancz, who had noted, as he himself writes, "well over a hundred minor passages about which I thought I should like to argue with Orwell." This foreword is included in the present first American edition of *The Road to Wigan Pier*.

FOREWORD

THIS FOREWORD is addressed to members of the Left
Book Club (to whom *The Road to Wigan Pier* is being sent
as the March Choice), and to them alone: members of
the general public are asked to ignore it. But for technical
considerations, it would have been deleted from the
ordinary edition.

I have also to make it clear that, while the three
selectors of the Left Book Club Choices—Strachey, Laski
and myself—were all agreed that a Foreword was desirable, I alone am responsible for what is written here—
though I think that Laski and Strachey would agree with
me.

Why did we think that a Foreword was desirable?
Because we find that many members—a surprisingly
large number—have the idea that in some sort of way a
Left Book Club Choice, first, represents the views of the
three selectors, and, secondly, incorporates the Left Book
Club " policy." A moment's thought should show that
the first suggestion could be true only in the worst kind
of Fascist State, and that the second is a contradiction in
terms: but we get letters so frequently—most interesting
and vital letters—which say: " Surely you and Laski and
Strachey cannot believe what So-and-So says on page
so-and-so of Such-and-Such a book," that there can
be no doubt at all that the misconception exists.

The plain facts are, of course, (a) that the three selectors, although they have that broad general agreement without which successful committee work is impossible, differ as to shade and *nuance* of opinion in a hundred ways; (b) that even if they were in perfect agreement on every point, nothing could be worse than a stream of books which expressed this same point of view over and over again; and (c) that their only criterion for a Choice is whether or not the reading and discussion of it will be helpful for the general struggle against Fascism and war. And that brings me on to this question of Left Book Club " policy." The Left Book Club has no " policy ": or rather it has no policy other than that of equipping people to fight against war and Fascism. As I have said elsewhere, it would not even be true to say that the People's Front is the " policy " of the Left Book Club, though all three selectors are enthusiastically in favour of it. What we rather feel is that by giving a wide distribution to books which represent many shades of Left opinion (and perhaps, most of all, by providing facilities for the discussion of those books in the 300 local centres and circles that have sprung up all over the country) we are creating the mass basis without which a genuine People's Front is impossible. In other words, the People's Front is not the " policy " of the Left Book Club, but the very existence of the Left Book Club tends towards a People's Front.

· · · · · · · ·

But we feel that a Foreword to *The Road to Wigan Pier* is desirable, not merely in view of the misconception to

which I have referred, but also because we believe that
the value of the book, for some members, can be greatly
increased if just a hint is given of certain vital considerations that arise from a reading of it. The value can be
increased: as to the positive value itself, no one of us has
the smallest doubt. For myself, it is a long time since I
have read so *living* a book, or one so full of a burning
indignation against poverty and oppression.

•   •   •   •   •   •   •   •   •

The plan of the book is this. In Part I Mr. Orwell
gives a first-hand account of the life of the working class
population of Wigan and elsewhere. It is a terrible record
of evil conditions, foul housing, wretched pay, hopeless
unemployment and the villainies of the Means Test: it
is also a tribute to courage and patience—patience far
too great. We cannot imagine anything more likely to
rouse the " unconverted " from their apathy than a
reading of this part of the book; and we are announcing
in the current number of *The Left News* a scheme by
means of which we hope members may make use of the
book for this end. These chapters really *are* the kind of
thing that makes converts.

In the second part, Mr. Orwell starts with an autobio-
graphical study, which he thinks necessary in order to
explain the class feelings and prejudices of a member of
" the lower upper-middle class," as he describes himself:
and he then goes on to declare his adherence to Socialism.
But before doing so he comes forward as a devil's
advocate, and explains, with a great deal of sympathy,

why, in his opinion, so many of the best people detest Socialism; and he finds the reason to lie in the " personal inferiority " of so many Socialists and in their mistaken methods of propaganda. His conclusion is that present methods should be thrown overboard, and that we should try to enrol everyone in the fight for Socialism and against Fascism and war (which he rightly sees to be disasters in the face of which little else is of much importance) by making the elemental appeal of " liberty " and " justice." What he envisages is a great league of " oppressed " against " oppressors "; in this battle members of all classes may fight side by side—the private schoolmaster and the jobless Cambridge graduate with the clerk and the unemployed miner; and then, when they have so fought, " we of the sinking middle class . . . may sink without further struggles into the working class where we belong, and probably when we get there it will not be so dreadful as we feared, for, after all, we have nothing to lose but our aitches."

　　·　　·　　·　　·　　·　　·　　·

Now the whole of this second part is highly provocative, not merely in its general argument, but also in detail after detail. I had, in point of fact, marked well over a hundred minor passages about which I thought I should like to argue with Mr. Orwell in this Foreword; but I find now that if I did so the space that I have set aside would be quickly used up, and I should wear out my readers' patience. It is necessary, therefore, that I should limit myself to some of the broader aspects.

In the first place, no reader must forget that Mr.

Orwell is throughout writing precisely as a member of the " lower upper-middle class " or, let us say without qualification, as a member of the middle class. It may seem stupid to insist on this point, as nothing could be clearer than Mr. Orwell's own insistence on it: but I can well imagine a reader coming across a remark every now and again which infuriates him even to the extent of making him forget this most important fact: *that such a remark can be made by Mr. Orwell is* (if the reader follows me) *part of Mr. Orwell's own case.* I have in mind in particular a lengthy passage in which Mr. Orwell embroiders the theme that, in the opinion of the middle class in general, the working class smells ! I believe myself that Mr. Orwell is exaggerating violently : I do not myself think that more than a very small proportion of them have this quaint idea (I admit that I may be a bad judge of the question, for I am a Jew, and passed the years of my early boyhood in a fairly close Jewish community; and, among Jews of this type, class distinctions do not exist—Mr. Orwell says that they do not exist among any sort of Oriental). But clearly *some* of them think like this—Mr. Orwell quotes a very odd passage from one of Mr. Somerset Maugham's books—and the whole of this chapter throws a most interesting light on the reality of class distinctions. I know, in fact, of no other book in which a member of the middle class exposes with such complete frankness the shameful way in which he was brought up to think of large numbers of his fellow men. This section will be, I think, of the greatest value to middle class and working class members of the Left Book Club alike: to the former because, if they are honest, they will search their own minds; to the latter, because it will make them understand what they are "up against"—if they do not understand it already. In any case, the moral is that the class division of Society, economic in origin, must be superseded by the classless society (I fear Mr. Orwell will regard this as a wretched and insincere cliché) in which alone the shame and indignity so vividly described by Mr. Orwell—I mean of the middle class, not of the lower class—will be impossible.

· · · · · · · · · ·

Mr. Orwell now proceeds to act as devil's advocate for the case against Socialism.

He looks at Socialists as a whole and finds them (with a few exceptions) a stupid, offensive and insincere lot. For my own part I find no similarity whatsoever between the picture as Mr. Orwell paints it and the picture as I see it. There is an extraordinary passage in which Mr. Orwell seems to suggest that almost every Socialist is a " crank "; and it is illuminating to discover from this passage just what Mr. Orwell means by the word. It appears to mean anyone holding opinions not held by the majority—for instance, any feminist, pacifist, vegetarian or advocate of birth control. This last is really startling. In the first part of the book Mr. Orwell paints a most vivid picture of wretched rooms swarming with children, and clearly becoming more and more unfit for human habitation the larger the family grows: but he apparently considers anyone who wishes to enlighten people as to how they can have a normal sexual life without increasing this misery as a crank ! The fact, of course, is that there is no more " commonsensical " work than that which is being done at the present time by the birth control clinics up and down the country—and common sense, as I understand it, is the antithesis of crankiness. I have chosen this particular example, because the answer to Mr. Orwell is to be found in his own first part: but the answers to Mr. Orwell's sneers at pacifism and feminism are as obvious. Even about vegetarianism (I apologise to vegetarians for the " even ") Mr. Orwell is astray. The majority of vegetarians are vegetarians not because " they want to add a few miserable years to their wretched lives " (I cannot find the exact passage at the moment, but that is roughly what Mr. Orwell says), but because they find something disgusting in the consumption of dead flesh. I am not saying that I agree with them : but anyone who has seen a man —or woman—eating a raw steak (*saignant*, as the French say so much more frankly) will feel a sneaking sympathy.

The fact is that in passages like that to which I have referred, and in numerous other places in this part of the book, Mr. Orwell is still a victim of that early atmosphere, in his home and public school, which he himself has so eloquently exposed. His conscience, his sense of decency, his understanding of realities tell him to declare himself a Socialist: but fighting against this compulsion there is in him all the time a compulsion far less conscious but almost—though fortunately not quite—as strong : the compulsion to conform to the mental habits

of his class. That is why Mr. Orwell, looking at a
Socialist, smells out (to use a word which we have already
met in another connection) a certain crankiness in him;
and he finds, as examples of this crankiness, a hatred of
war (pacifism), a desire to see woman no longer oppressed
by men (feminism), and a refusal to withhold the knowledge which will add a little happiness to certain human
lives (birth control).

This conflict of two compulsions is to be found again
and again throughout the book. For instance, Mr. Orwell
calls himself a " half intellectual "; but the truth is that
he is at one and the same time an extreme intellectual
and a violent anti-intellectual. Similarly he is a frightful
snob—still (he must forgive me for saying this), and a
genuine hater of every form of snobbery. For those who
can read, the exhibition of this conflict is neither the
least interesting nor the least valuable part of the book:
for it shows the desperate struggle through which a man
must go before, in our present society, his mind can
really become free—if indeed that is ever possible.

I have said enough, I think, to show, by means of one
example, the way in which I should venture to criticise
the whole of this section of the book. But there is
another topic here which cannot be passed over without
a word or two. Among the grave faults which Mr. Orwell
finds in Socialist propaganda is the glorification of industrialism, and in particular of the triumphs of industrialisation in the Soviet Union (the words "Magnitogorsk"
and " Dnieper " make Mr. Orwell see red—or rather the
reverse). I have a fairly wide acquaintance among

Socialists of every colour, and I feel sure that the whole
of this section is based on a misunderstanding. To leave
Russia out of account for the moment, no Socialist of my
acquaintance *glorifies* industrialism. What the Socialist
who has advanced beyond the most elementary stage
says (and I really mean what he *says*, not what he *ought
to say*) is that capitalist industrialism is a certain stage
which we have reached in the business of providing for
our needs, comforts and luxuries: that though it may be
amusing to speculate on whether or not a pre-indus-
trialist civilisation might be a more attractive one in
which to live, it is a matter of plain common sense that,
whatever individuals may wish, industrialism will go on:
that (if Mr. Orwell will forgive the jargon) such " contradictions " have developed in the machine of capitalist
industrialism that the thing is visibly breaking down:
that such break-down means poverty, unemployment
and war: and that the only solution is the supersession
of anarchic capitalist industrialism by planned Socialist
industrialism. In other words, it is not industrialism that
the Socialist advocates (a man does not advocate the sun
or the moon), but Socialist industrialism as opposed to
capitalist industrialism.

Mr. Orwell, of course, understands this quite elementary fact perfectly well: but his understanding conflicts
with his love of beauty, and the result is that, instead of
pointing out that industrialism can be the parent of
beauty, if at all, then only under planned Socialist industrialism, he turns to rend the mythical figure of the
Socialist who thinks that gaspipe chairs are more

beautiful than Chippendale chairs. (Incidentally, gaspipe chairs *are* more beautiful than the worst Chippendale chairs, though not nearly as beautiful as the
best.)

As to the particular question of the Soviet Union, the
insistence of Socialists on the achievements of Soviet industrialisation arises from the fact that the most frequent
argument which Socialists have to face is precisely this:
" I agree with you that Socialism would be wholly
admirable if it would work—but it wouldn't." Somewhere or other Mr. Orwell speaks of intelligent and
unintelligent Socialists, and brushes aside people who
say " it wouldn't work " as belonging to the latter category. My own experience is that this is still the major
sincere objection to Socialism on the part of decent people,
and the major *insincere* objection on the part of indecent
people who in fact are thinking of their dividends. It is
true that the objection was more frequently heard in
1919 than in 1927, in 1927 than at the end of the first
Five Year Plan, and at the end of the first Five Year
Plan than to-day—the reason being precisely that quite so
direct a *non possumus* hardly carries conviction, when the
achievements of the Soviet Union are there for everyone
to see. But people will go on hypnotising themselves and
others with a formula, even when that formula is
patently outworn: so that it is still necessary, and will
be necessary for a long time yet, to show that modern
methods of production *do* work under Socialism and *no
longer work* under capitalism.

But Mr. Orwell's attack on Socialists who are for ever

singing pæans of praise to Soviet industrialisation is also connected with his general dislike of Russia—he even commits the curious indiscretion of referring to Russian commissars as " half-gramophones, half-gangsters." Here again the particular nature of Mr. Orwell's unresolved conflict is not difficult to understand; nor is it difficult to understand why Mr. Orwell states that almost all people of real sensitiveness, and in particular almost all writers and artists and the like, are hostile to Socialism—whereas the truth is that in several countries, for instance in France, a great number, and probably the majority, of writers and artists are Socialists or even Communists.

All this is not to say that (while this section gives, in my view, a distorted picture of what Socialists are like and what they say) *Socialists themselves* will not find there much that is of value to them, and many shrewd pieces of, at any rate, half-truth. In particular I think that Mr. Orwell's accusation of arrogance and dogmatism is to a large extent justified: in fact as I think back on what I have already written here I am not sure that a good deal of it is not itself arrogant and dogmatic. His accusation of narrowness and of sectarianism is not so well grounded to-day as it would have been a few years ago: but here also there is still plenty of room for improvement. The whole section indeed is, when all has been said against it, a challenge to us Socialists to put our house and our characters in order.

· · · · · · · · ·

Having criticised us in this way (for though Mr. Orwell insists that he is speaking merely as devil's advocate and saying what other people say, quite often and quite obviously he is really speaking *in propria persona*—or perhaps I had better say "in his own person," otherwise Mr. Orwell will class me with "the snobs who write in Latinised English" or words to that effect) Mr. Orwell joins us generously and whole-heartedly, but begs us to drop our present methods of propaganda, to base our appeal on freedom and liberty, and to see ourselves as a league of the oppressed against the oppressors. Nothing could be more admirable as a first approach; and I agree that we shall never mobilise that vast mass of fundamentally decent opinion which undoubtedly exists (as, for instance, the Peace Ballot showed) and which we *must* mobilise if we are to defeat Fascism, unless we make our first appeal to its generous impulses. It is from a desire for liberty and justice that we must draw our militant strength; and the society which we are trying to establish is one in which that liberty and that justice will be incarnate. But between the beginning in that first impulse to fight, and the end when, the fight won, our children or our children's children will live in the achievement, there is a great deal of hard work and hard thinking to be done—less noble and more humdrum than the appeal to generosities, but no less important if a real victory is to be won, and if this very appeal is not to be used to serve ends quite opposite to those at which we aim.

It is indeed significant that so far as I can remember (he must forgive me if I am mistaken) Mr. Orwell does not once define what he *means* by Socialism; nor does he explain *how* the oppressors oppress, nor even what he understands by the words " liberty " and "justice." I hope he will not think I am quibbling: he will not, I think, if he remembers that the word " Nazi " is an abbreviation of the words " National Socialist "; that in its first phase Fascism draws its chief strength from an attack on " oppression "—" oppression " by capitalists, multiple stores, Jews and foreigners; that no word is commoner in German speeches to-day than " Justice "; and that if you " listen in " any night to Berlin or Munich, the chances are that you will hear the " liberty " of totalitarian Germany—" Germans have become free by becoming a united people "—compared with the misery of Stalin's slaves.

What is indeed essential, once that first appeal has been made to " liberty " and "justice," is a careful and patient study of just *how* the thing works: of *why* capitalism inevitably means oppression and injustice and the horrible class society which Mr. Orwell so brilliantly depicts: of *the means* of transition to a Socialist society in which there will be neither oppressor nor oppressed. In other words, *emotional* Socialism must become scientific Socialism—even if some of us have to concern ourselves with what Mr. Orwell, in his extremely intellectualist anti-intellectualism, calls " the sacred sisters " Thesis, Antithesis and Synthesis.

What I feel, in sum, is that this book, more perhaps than any that the Left Book Club has issued, clarifies —for me at least—the whole meaning and purpose of the Club. On the one hand we have to go out and rouse the apathetic by showing them the utter vileness which Mr. Orwell lays bare in the first part of the book, and by appealing to the decency which is in them; on the other hand we have so to equip ourselves by thought and study that we run no danger, having once mobilised all this good will, of seeing it dispersed for lack of trained leaders—lance corporals as well as generals—or even of seeing it used as the shock troops of our enemies.

V. G.

January 11th, 1937.

THE ROAD TO WIGAN PIER

PART I

CHAPTER I

THE FIRST SOUND in the mornings was the clumping of the mill-girls' clogs down the cobbled street. Earlier than that, I suppose, there were factory whistles which I was never awake to hear.

There were generally four of us in the bedroom, and a beastly place it was, with that defiled impermanent look of rooms that are not serving their rightful purpose. Years earlier the house had been an ordinary dwelling-house, and when the Brookers had taken it and fitted it out as a tripe-shop and lodging-house, they had inherited some of the more useless pieces of furniture and had never had the energy to remove them. We were therefore sleeping in what was still recognisably a drawing-room. Hanging from the ceiling there was a heavy glass chandelier on which the dust was so thick that it was like fur. And covering most of one wall there was a huge hideous piece of junk, something between a sideboard and a hall-stand, with lots of carving and little drawers and strips of looking-glass, and there was a once-gaudy carpet ringed by the slop-pails of years, and two gilt chairs with burst seats, and one of those old-fashioned horsehair armchairs which you slide off when you try to sit on them. The room had been turned into a bedroom by thrusting four squalid beds in among this other wreckage.

My bed was in the right-hand corner on the side nearest the door. There was another bed across the foot of it and jammed hard against it (it had to be in that position to allow the door to open) so that I had to sleep with my legs doubled up; if I straightened them out I kicked the occupant of the other bed in the small of the back. He was an elderly man named Mr. Reilly, a mechanic of sorts and employed " on top " at one of the coal-pits. Luckily he had to go to work at five in the morning, so I could uncoil my legs and have a couple of hours' proper sleep after he was gone. In the bed oppo-site there was a Scotch miner who had been injured in a pit accident (a huge chunk of stone pinned him to the ground and it was a couple of hours before they could lever it off), and had received five hundred pounds compensation. He was a big handsome man of forty, with grizzled hair and a clipped moustache, more like a sergeant-major than a miner, and he would lie in bed till late in the day, smoking a short pipe. The other bed was occupied by a succession of commercial travellers, newspaper-canvassers and hire-purchase touts who generally stayed for a couple of nights. It was a double bed and much the best in the room. I had slept in it myself my first night there, but had been manœuvred out of it to make room for another lodger. I believe all newcomers spent their first night in the double bed, which was used, so to speak, as bait. All the windows were kept tight shut, with a red sandbag jammed in the bottom, and in the morning the room stank like a ferret's cage. You did not notice it when you got up, but if you went out of the room and came back, the smell hit you in the face with a smack.

I never discovered how many bedrooms the house contained, but strange to say there was a bathroom, dating from before the Brookers' time. Downstairs there was the usual kitchen living-room with its huge open range burning night and day. It was lighted only by a skylight, for on one side of it was the shop and on the other the larder, which opened into some dark subterranean place where the tripe was stored. Partly blocking the door of the larder there was a shapeless sofa upon which Mrs. Brooker, our landlady, lay permanently ill, festooned in grimy blankets. She had a big, pale yellow, anxious face. No one knew for certain what was the matter with her; I suspect that her only real trouble was over-eating. In front of the fire there was almost always a line of damp washing, and in the middle of the room was the big kitchen table at which the family and all the lodgers ate. I never saw this table completely uncovered, but I saw its various wrappings at different times. At the bottom there was a layer of old newspapers stained by Worcester Sauce; above that a sheet of sticky white oilcloth; above that a green serge cloth; above that a coarse linen cloth, never changed and seldom taken off. Generally the crumbs from breakfast were still on the table at supper. I used to get to know individual crumbs by sight and watch their progress up and down the table from day to day.

The shop was a narrow, cold sort of room. On the outside of the window a few white letters, relics of ancient chocolate advertisements, were scattered like stars. Inside there was a slab upon which lay the great white folds of tripe, and the grey flocculent stuff known as " black tripe," and the ghostly translucent feet of pigs, ready boiled. It was the ordinary " tripe and pea " shop, and not much else was stocked except bread, cigarettes and tinned stuff. " Teas " were advertised in the window, but if a customer demanded a cup of tea he was usually put off with excuses. Mr. Brooker, though out of work for two years, was a miner by trade, but he and his wife had been keeping shops of various kinds as a side-line all their lives. At one time they had had a pub, but they had lost their licence for allowing gambling on the premises. I doubt whether any of their businesses had ever paid; they were the kind of people who run a business chiefly in order to have something to grumble about. Mr. Brooker was a dark, small-boned, sour, Irish-looking man, and astonishingly dirty. I don't think I ever once saw his hands clean. As Mrs. Brooker was now an invalid he prepared most of the food, and like all people with permanently dirty hands he had a peculiarly intimate, lingering manner of handling things. If he gave you a slice of bread-and-butter there was always a black thumb-print on it. Even in the early morning when he descended into the mysterious den behind Mrs. Brooker's sofa and fished out the tripe, his hands were already black. I heard dreadful stories from the other lodgers about the place where the tripe was kept. Blackbeetles were said to swarm there. I do not know how often fresh consignments of tripe were ordered, but it was at long intervals, for Mrs. Brooker used to date events by it. " Let me see now, I've had in three lots of froze (frozen tripe) since that happened," etc., etc. We lodgers were never given tripe to eat. At the time I imagined that this was because tripe was too expensive; I have since thought that it was merely because we knew too much about it. The Brookers never ate tripe themselves, I noticed.

The only permanent lodgers were the Scotch miner, Mr. Reilly, two old-age pensioners and an unemployed man on the P.A.C. named Joe—he was the kind of person who has no surname. The Scotch miner was a bore when you got to know him. Like so many unemployed men he spent too much time reading newspapers, and if you did not head him off he would discourse for hours about such things as the Yellow Peril, trunk murders, astrology, and the conflict between religion and science. The old-age pensioners had, as usual, been driven from their homes by the Means Test. They handed their weekly ten shillings over to the Brookers and in return got the kind of accommodation you would expect for ten shillings; that is, a bed in the attic and meals chiefly of bread-and-butter. One of them was of " superior " type and was dying of some malignant disease—cancer, I believe. He only got out of bed on the days when he went to draw his pension. The other, called by everyone Old Jack, was an ex-miner aged seventy-eight who had worked well over fifty years in the pits. He was alert and intelligent, but curiously enough he seemed only to remember his boyhood experiences and to have forgotten all about the modern mining machinery and improvements. He used to tell me tales of fights with savage horses in the narrow galleries underground. When he heard that I was arranging to go down several coal mines he was contemptuous and declared that a man of my size (six feet two and a half) would never manage the " travelling "; it was no use telling him that the " travelling " was better than it used to be. But he was friendly to everyone and used to give us all a fine shout of " Good night, boys ! " as he crawled up the stairs to his bed somewhere under the rafters. What I most admired about Old Jack was that he never cadged; he was generally out of tobacco towards the end of the week, but he always refused to smoke anyone else's. The Brookers had insured the lives of both old-age pensioners with one of the tanner-a-week companies. It was said that they were overheard anxiously asking the insurance-tout " how long people lived when they'd got cancer."

Joe, like the Scotchman, was a great reader of newspapers and spent almost his entire day in the public
library. He was the typical unmarried unemployed
man, a derelict-looking, frankly ragged creature with a
round, almost childish face on which there was a naïvely
naughty expression. He looked more like a neglected
little boy than a grown-up man. I suppose it is the
complete lack of responsibility that makes so many of
these men look younger than their ages. From Joe's
appearance I took him to be about twenty-eight, and
was amazed to learn that he was forty-three. He had a
love of resounding phrases and was very proud of the
astuteness with which he had avoided getting married.
He often said to me, " Matrimonial chains is a big
item," evidently feeling this to be a very subtle and por-
tentous remark. His total income was fifteen shillings a
week, and he paid out six or seven to the Brookers for his
bed. I sometimes used to see him making himself a cup of
tea over the kitchen fire, but for the rest he got his meals
somewhere out of doors; it was mostly slices of bread-
and-marg and packets of fish and chips, I suppose.

Besides these there was a floating clientele of commercial travellers of the poorer sort, travelling actors
—always common in the North because most of the
larger pubs hire variety artists at the week-ends—and
newspaper-canvassers. The newspaper-canvassers were
a type I had never met before. Their job seemed to me
so hopeless, so appalling that I wondered how anyone
could put up with such a thing when prison was a
possible alternative. They were employed mostly by
weekly or Sunday papers, and they were sent from
town to town, provided with maps and given a list of
streets which they had to " work " each day. If they
failed to secure a minimum of twenty orders a day,

they got the sack. So long as they kept up their twenty orders a day they received a small salary—two pounds a week, I think; on any order over the twenty they drew a tiny commission. The thing is not so impossible as it sounds, because in working-class districts every family takes in a twopenny weekly paper and changes it every few weeks; but I doubt whether anyone keeps a job of that kind long. The newspapers engage poor desperate wretches, out-of-work clerks and commercial travellers and the like, who for a while make frantic efforts and keep their sales up to the minimum; then as the deadly work wears them down they are sacked and fresh men are taken on. I got to know two who were employed by one of the more notorious weeklies. Both of them were middle-aged men with families to support, and one of them was a grandfather. They were on their feet ten hours a day, "working" their appointed streets, and then busy late into the night filling in blank forms for some swindle their paper was running —one of those schemes by which you are " given " a set of crockery if you take out a six weeks' subscription and send a two-shilling postal order as well. The fat one, the grandfather, used to fall asleep with his head on a pile of forms. Neither of them could afford the pound a week which the Brookers charged for full board. They used to pay a small sum for their beds and make shame-faced meals in a corner of the kitchen off bacon and bread-and-margarine which they stored in their suit-cases.

The Brookers had large numbers of sons and daughters, most of whom had long since fled from home. Some were in Canada—" at Canada," as Mrs. Brooker used to put it. There was only one son living near by, a large pig-like young man employed in a garage, who frequently came to the house for his meals. His wife was there all day with the two children, and most of the cooking and laundering was done by her and by Emmie, the fiancée of another son who was in London. Emmie was a fair-haired, sharp-nosed, unhappy-looking girl who worked at one of the mills for some starvation wage, but nevertheless spent all her evenings in bondage at the Brookers' house. I gathered that the marriage was constantly being postponed and would probably never take place, but Mrs. Brooker had already appropriated Emmie as a daughter-in-law, and nagged her in that peculiar watchful, loving way that invalids have. The rest of the housework was done, or not done, by Mr. Brooker. Mrs. Brooker seldom rose from her sofa in the kitchen (she spent the night there as well as the day) and was too ill to do anything except eat stupendous meals. It was Mr. Brooker who attended to the shop, gave the lodgers their food and " did out " the bedrooms. He was always moving with incredible slowness from one hated job to another. Often the beds were still unmade at six in the evening, and at any hour of the day you were liable to meet Mr. Brooker on the stairs, carrying a full chamber-pot which he gripped with his thumb well over the rim. In the mornings he sat by the fire with a tub of filthy water, peeling potatoes at the speed of a slow-motion picture. I never saw anyone who could peel potatoes with quite such an air of brooding resentment. You could see the hatred of this " bloody woman's work," as he called it, fermenting inside him, a kind of bitter juice. He was one of those people who can chew their grievances like a cud.

Of course, as I was indoors a good deal, I heard all about the Brookers' woes, and how everyone swindled them and was ungrateful to them, and how the shop did not pay and the lodging-house hardly paid. By local standards they were not so badly off, for, in some way I did not understand, Mr. Brooker was dodging the Means Test and drawing an allowance from the P.A.C., but their chief pleasure was talking about their grievances to anyone who would listen. Mrs. Brooker used to lament by the hour, lying on her sofa, a soft mound of fat and self-pity, saying the same things over and over again. " We don't seem to get no customers nowadays. I don't know 'ow it is. The tripe's just a-laying there day after day—such beautiful tripe it is, too ! It does seem 'ard, don't it now ? " etc., etc., etc. All Mrs. Brooker's laments ended with " It does seem 'ard, don't it now ? " like the refrain of a ballade. Certainly it was true that the shop did not pay. The whole place had the unmistakable dusty, flyblown air of a business that is going down. But it would have been quite useless to explain to them *why* nobody came to the shop, even if one had had the face to do it; neither was capable of understanding that last year's dead blue-bottles supine in the shop window, are not good for trade.

But the thing that really tormented them was the thought of those two old-age pensioners living in their house, usurping floor-space, devouring food and paying only ten shillings a week. I doubt whether they were really losing money over the old-age pensioners, though certainly the profit on ten shillings a week must have been very small. But in their eyes the two old men were a kind of dreadful parasite who had fastened on them and were living on their charity. Old Jack they could just tolerate, because he kept out-of-doors most of the day, but they really hated the bedridden one, Hooker

by name. Mr. Brooker had a queer way of pronouncing
his name, without the H and with a long U—" Uker."
What tales I heard about old Hooker and his fractious-
ness, the nuisance of making his bed, the way he
" wouldn't eat " this and " wouldn't eat " that, his
endless ingratitude and, above all, the selfish obstinacy
with which he refused to die ! The Brookers were quite
openly pining for him to die. When that happened they
could at least draw the insurance money. They seemed
to feel him there, eating their substance day after day,
as though he had been a living worm in their bowels.
Sometimes Mr. Brooker would look up from his potato-
peeling, catch my eye and jerk his head with a look
of inexpressible bitterness towards the ceiling, towards
old Hooker's room. " It's a b——, ain't it ? " he would
say. There was no need to say more; I had heard all
about old Hooker's ways already. But the Brookers had
grievances of one kind and another against all their
lodgers, myself included, no doubt. Joe, being on the
P.A.C., was practically in the same category as the old-
age pensioners. The Scotchman paid a pound a week,
but he was indoors most of the day and they " didn't
like him always hanging round the place," as they put
it. The newspaper-canvassers were out all day, but the
Brookers bore them a grudge for bringing in their own
food, and even Mr. Reilly, their best lodger, was in
disgrace because Mrs. Brooker said that he woke her
up when he came downstairs in the mornings. They
couldn't, they complained perpetually, get the kind of
lodgers they wanted—good-class " commercial gentlemen " who paid full board and were out all day. Their
ideal lodger would have been somebody who paid
thirty shillings a week and never came indoors except
to sleep. I have noticed that people who let lodgings

nearly always hate their lodgers. They want their money but they look on them as intruders and have a curiously watchful, jealous attitude which at bottom is a determination not to let the lodger make himself too much at home. It is an inevitable result of the bad system by which the lodger has to live in somebody else's house without being one of the family.

The meals at the Brookers' house were uniformly disgusting. For breakfast you got two rashers of bacon and a pale fried egg, and bread-and-butter which had often been cut overnight and always had thumb-marks on it. However tactfully I tried, I could never induce Mr. Brooker to let me cut my own bread-and-butter; he *would* hand it to me slice by slice, each slice gripped firmly under that broad black thumb. For dinner there were generally those threepenny steak puddings which are sold ready-made in tins—these were part of the stock of the shop, I think—and boiled potatoes and rice pudding. For tea there was more bread-and-butter and frayed-looking sweet cakes which were probably bought as " stales " from the baker. For supper there was the pale flabby Lancashire cheese and biscuits. The Brookers never called these biscuits biscuits. They always referred to them reverently as " cream crackers "—" Have another cream cracker, Mr. Reilly. You'll like a cream cracker with your cheese "—thus glozing over the fact that there was only cheese for supper. Several bottles of Worcester Sauce and a half-full jar of marmalade lived permanently on the table. It was usual to souse everything, even a piece of cheese, with Worcester Sauce, but I never saw anyone brave the marmalade jar, which was an unspeakable mass of stickiness and dust. Mrs. Brooker had her meals separately but also took snacks from any meal that happened to be going, and manœuvred with great skill for what she called " the bottom of the pot," meaning the strongest cup of tea. She had a habit of constantly wiping her mouth on one of her blankets. Towards the end of my stay she took to tearing off strips of newspaper for this purpose, and in the morning the floor was often littered with crumpled-up balls of slimy paper which lay there for hours. The smell of the kitchen was dreadful, but, as with that of the bedroom, you ceased to notice it after a while.

It struck me that this place must be fairly normal as lodging-houses in the industrial areas go, for on the whole the lodgers did not complain. The only one who ever did so to my knowledge was a little black-haired, sharp-nosed Cockney, a traveller for a cigarette firm. He had never been in the North before, and I think that till recently he had been in better employ and was used to staying in commercial hotels. This was his first glimpse of really low-class lodgings, the kind of place in which the poor tribe of touts and canvassers have to shelter upon their endless journeys. In the morning as we were dressing (he had slept in the double bed, of course) I saw him look round the desolate room with a sort of wondering aversion. He caught my eye and suddenly divined that I was a fellow-Southerner.

" The filthy bloody bastards ! " he said feelingly.

After that he packed his suit-case, went downstairs and, with great strength of mind, told the Brookers that this was not the kind of house he was accustomed to and that he was leaving immediately. The Brookers could never understand why. They were astonished and hurt. The ingratitude of it ! Leaving them like that for no reason after a single night ! Afterwards they discussed it over and over again, in all its bearings. It was added to their store of grievances.

On the day when there was a full chamber-pot under the breakfast table I decided to leave. The place was beginning to depress me. It was not only the dirt, the smells and the vile food, but the feeling of stagnant meaningless decay, of having got down into some subterranean place where people go creeping round and round, just like blackbeetles, in an endless muddle of slovened jobs and mean grievances. The most dreadful thing about people like the Brookers is the way they say the same things over and over again. It gives you the feeling that they are not real people at all, but a kind of ghost for ever rehearsing the same futile rigmarole. In the end Mrs. Brooker's self-pitying talk—always the same complaints, over and over, and always ending with the tremulous whine of " It does seem 'ard, don't it now ? " —revolted me even more than her habit of wiping her mouth with bits of newspaper. But it is no use saying that people like the Brookers are just disgusting and trying to put them out of mind. For they exist in tens and hundreds of thousands; they are one of the characteristic by-products of the modern world. You cannot disregard them if you accept the civilisation that produced them. For this is part at least of what industrialism has done for us. Columbus sailed the Atlantic, the first steam engines tottered into motion, the British squares stood firm under the French guns at Waterloo, the one-eyed scoundrels of the nineteenth century praised God and filled their pockets; and this is where it all led—to labyrinthine slums and dark back kitchens with sickly, ageing people creeping round and round them like blackbeetles. It is a kind of duty to see and smell such places now and again, especially smell them, lest you should forget that they exist; though perhaps it is better not to stay there too long.

The train bore me away, through the monstrous scenery of slag-heaps, chimneys, piled scrap-iron, foul canals, paths of cindery mud criss-crossed by the prints of clogs. This was March, but the weather had been horribly cold and everywhere there were mounds of blackened snow. As we moved slowly through the out-skirts of the town we passed row after row of little grey slum houses running at right angles to the embankment. At the back of one of the houses a young woman was kneeling on the stones, poking a stick up the leaden waste-pipe which ran from the sink inside and which I suppose was blocked. I had time to see everything about her—her sacking apron, her clumsy clogs, her arms red-dened by the cold. She looked up as the train passed, and I was almost near enough to catch her eye. She had a round pale face, the usual exhausted face of the slum girl who is twenty-five and looks forty, thanks to mis-carriages and drudgery; and it wore, for the second in which I saw it, the most desolate, hopeless expression I have ever seen. It struck me then that we are mistaken when we say that " It isn't the same for them as it would be for us," and that people bred in the slums can imagine nothing but the slums. For what I saw in her face was not the ignorant suffering of an animal. She knew well enough what was happening to her—understood as well as I did how dreadful a destiny it was to be kneeling there in the bitter cold, on the slimy stones of a slum backyard, poking a stick up a foul drain-pipe.

But quite soon the train drew away into open country, and that seemed strange, almost unnatural, as though the open country had been a kind of park; for in the industrial areas one always feels that the smoke and filth must go on for ever and that no part of the earth's surface can escape them. In a crowded, dirty little country like ours one takes defilement almost for granted. Slag-heaps and chimneys seem a more normal, probable landscape than grass and trees, and even in the depths of the country when you drive your fork into the ground you half expect to lever up a broken bottle or a rusty can. But out here the snow was untrodden and lay so deep that only the tops of the stone boundary-walls were showing, winding over the hills like black paths. I remembered that D. H. Lawrence, writing of this same landscape or another near by, said that the snow-covered hills rippled away into the distance "like muscle." It was not the simile that would have occurred to me. To my eye the snow and the black walls were more like a white dress with black piping running across it.

Although the snow was hardly broken the sun was shining brightly, and behind the shut windows of the carriage it seemed warm. According to the almanac this was spring, and a few of the birds seemed to believe it. For the first time in my life, in a bare patch beside the line, I saw rooks treading. They did it on the ground and not, as I should have expected, in a tree. The manner of courtship was curious. The female stood with her beak open and the male walked round her and appeared to be feeding her. I had hardly been in the train half an hour, but it seemed a very long way from the Brookers' back-kitchen to the empty slopes of snow, the bright sunshine and the big gleaming birds.

The whole of the industrial districts are really one enormous town, of about the same population as Greater London but, fortunately, of much larger area; so that even in the middle of them there is still room for patches of cleanness and decency. That is an encouraging thought. In spite of hard trying, man has not yet succeeded in doing his dirt everywhere. The earth is so vast

and still so empty that even in the filthy heart of civilisation you find fields where the grass is green instead of
grey; perhaps if you looked for them you might even
find streams with live fish in them instead of salmon tins.
For quite a long time, perhaps another twenty minutes,
the train was rolling through open country before the
villa-civilisation began to close in upon us again, and
then the outer slums, and then the slag-heaps, belching
chimneys, blast-furnaces, canals and gasometers of
another industrial town.

CHAPTER II

OUR CIVILISATION, *pace* Chesterton, *is* founded on coal, more completely than one realises until one stops to think about it. The machines that keep us alive, and the machines that make the machines, are all directly or indirectly dependent upon coal. In the metabolism of the Western world the coal-miner is second in importance only to the man who ploughs the soil. He is a sort of grimy caryatid upon whose shoulders nearly everything that is *not* grimy is supported. For this reason the actual process by which coal is extracted is well worth watching, if you get the chance and are willing to take the trouble.

When you go down a coal-mine it is important to try and get to the coal face when the " fillers " are at work. This is not easy, because when the mine is working visitors are a nuisance and are not encouraged, but if you go at any other time, it is possible to come away with a totally wrong impression. On a Sunday, for instance, a mine seems almost peaceful. The time to go there is when the machines are roaring and the air is black with coal dust, and when you can actually see what the miners have to do. At those times the place is like hell, or at any rate like my own mental picture of hell. Most of the things one imagines in hell are there—heat, noise, confusion, darkness, foul air, and, above all, unbearably cramped space. Everything except the fire, for there is no fire down there except the feeble beams of

Davy lamps and electric torches which scarcely penetrate the clouds of coal dust.

When you have finally got there—and getting there is a job in itself: I will explain that in a moment—you crawl through the last line of pit props and see opposite you a shiny black wall three or four feet high. This is the coal face. Overhead is the smooth ceiling made by the rock from which the coal has been cut; underneath is the rock again, so that the gallery you are in is only as high as the ledge of coal itself, probably not much more than a yard. The first impression of all, overmastering everything else for a while, is the frightful, deafening din from the conveyor belt which carries the coal away. You cannot see very far, because the fog of coal dust throws back the beam of your lamp, but you can see on either side of you the line of half-naked kneeling men, one to every four or five yards, driving their shovels under the fallen coal and flinging it swiftly over their left shoulders. They are feeding it on to the conveyor belt, a moving rubber belt a couple of feet wide which runs a yard or two behind them. Down this belt a glittering river of coal races constantly. In a big mine it is carrying away several tons of coal every minute. It bears it off to some place in the main roads where it is shot into tubs holding half a ton, and thence dragged to the cages and hoisted to the outer air.

It is impossible to watch the " fillers " at work without feeling a pang of envy for their toughness. It is a dreadful job that they do, an almost superhuman job by the standards of an ordinary person. For they are not only shifting monstrous quantities of coal, they are also doing it in a position that doubles or trebles the work. They have got to remain kneeling all the while—they could hardly rise from their knees without hitting the ceiling—

and you can easily see by trying it what a tremendous effort this means. Shovelling is comparatively easy when you are standing up, because you can use your knee and thigh to drive the shovel along; kneeling down, the whole of the strain is thrown upon your arm and belly muscles. And the other conditions do not exactly make things easier. There is the heat—it varies, but in some mines it is suffocating—and the coal dust that stuffs up your throat and nostrils and collects along your eyelids, and the unending rattle of the conveyor belt, which in that confined space is rather like the rattle of a machine gun. But the fillers look and work as though they were made of iron. They really do look like iron—hammered iron statues—under the smooth coat of coal dust which clings to them from head to foot. It is only when you see miners down the mine and naked that you realise what splendid men they are. Most of them are small (big men are at a disadvantage in that job) but nearly all of them have the most noble bodies; wide shoulders tapering to slender supple waists, and small pronounced buttocks and sinewy thighs, with not an ounce of waste flesh anywhere. In the hotter mines they wear only a pair of thin drawers, clogs and knee-pads; in the hottest mines of all, only the clogs and knee-pads. You can hardly tell by the look of them whether they are young or old. They may be any age up to sixty or even sixty-five, but when they are black and naked they all look alike. No one could do their work who had not a young man's body, and a figure fit for a guardsman at that; just a few pounds of extra flesh on the waist-line, and the constant bending would be impossible. You can never forget that spectacle once you have seen it—the line of bowed, kneeling figures, sooty black all over, driving their huge shovels under the coal with stupendous force and speed. They are on the job for seven and a half hours, theoretically without a break, for there is no time " off." Actually they snatch a quarter of an hour or so at some time during the shift to eat the food they have brought with them, usually a hunk of bread and dripping and a bottle of cold tea. The first time I was watching the " fillers " at work I put my hand upon some dreadful slimy thing among the coal dust. It was a chewed quid of tobacco. Nearly all the miners chew tobacco, which is said to be good against thirst.

Probably you have to go down several coal-mines before you can get much grasp of the processes that are going on round you. This is chiefly because the mere effort of getting from place to place makes it difficult to notice anything else. In some ways it is even disappointing, or at least is unlike what you have expected. You get into the cage, which is a steel box about as wide as a telephone box and two or three times as long. It holds ten men, but they pack it like pilchards in a tin, and a tall man cannot stand upright in it. The steel door shuts upon you, and somebody working the winding gear above drops you into the void. You have the usual momentary qualm in your belly and a bursting sensation in the ears, but not much sensation of movement till you get near the bottom, when the cage slows down so abruptly that you could swear it is going upwards again. In the middle of the run the cage probably touches sixty miles an hour; in some of the deeper mines it touches even more. When you crawl out at the bottom you are perhaps four hundred yards under ground. That is to say you have a tolerable-sized mountain on top of you; hundreds of yards of solid rock, bones of extinct beasts, subsoil, flints, roots of growing things, green grass and cows grazing on it—all this suspended over your head and held back only by wooden props as thick as the calf of your leg. But because of the speed at which the cage has brought you down, and the complete blackness through which you have travelled, you hardly feel yourself deeper down than you would at the bottom of the Piccadilly tube.

What *is* surprising, on the other hand, is the immense horizontal distances that have to be travelled underground. Before I had been down a mine I had vaguely imagined the miner stepping out of the cage and getting to work on a ledge of coal a few yards away. I had not realised that before he even gets to his work he may have to creep through passages as long as from London Bridge to Oxford Circus. In the beginning, of course, a mine shaft is sunk somewhere near a seam of coal. But as that seam is worked out and fresh seams are followed up, the workings get further and further from the pit bottom. If it is a mile from the pit bottom to the coal face, that is probably an average distance; three miles is a fairly normal one; there are even said to be a few mines where it is as much as five miles. But these distances bear no relation to distances above ground. For in all that mile or three miles as it may be, there is hardly anywhere outside the main road, and not many places even there, where a man can stand upright.

You do not notice the effect of this till you have gone a few hundred yards. You start off, stooping slightly, down the dim-lit gallery, eight or ten feet wide and about five high, with the walls built up with slabs of shale, like the stone walls in Derbyshire. Every yard or two there are wooden props holding up the beams and girders; some of the girders have buckled into fantastic curves under which you have to duck. Usually it is bad going underfoot—thick dust or jagged chunks of shale, and in some mines where there is water it is as mucky as a farm-yard. Also there is the track for the coal tubs, like a miniature railway track with sleepers a foot or two apart, which is tiresome to walk on. Everything is grey with shale dust; there is a dusty fiery smell which seems to be the same in all mines. You see mysterious machines of which you never learn the purpose, and bundles of tools slung together on wires, and sometimes mice darting away from the beam of the lamps. They are surprisingly common, especially in mines where there are or have been horses. It would be interesting to know how they got there in the first place; possibly by falling down the shaft—for they say a mouse can fall any distance uninjured, owing to its surface area being so large relative to its weight. You press yourself against the wall to make way for lines of tubs jolting slowly towards the shaft, drawn by an endless steel cable operated from the surface. You creep through sacking curtains and thick wooden doors which, when they are opened, let out fierce blasts of air. These doors are an important part of the ventilation system. The exhausted air is sucked out of one shaft by means of fans, and the fresh air enters the other of its own accord. But if left to itself the air will take the shortest way round, leaving the deeper workings unventilated; so all short cuts have to be partitioned off.

At the start to walk stooping is rather a joke, but it is a joke that soon wears off. I am handicapped by being exceptionally tall, but when the roof falls to four feet or less it is a tough job for anybody except a dwarf or a child. You have not only got to bend double, you have also got to keep your head up all the while so as to see the beams and girders and dodge them when they come You have, therefore, a constant crick in the neck, but this is nothing to the pain in your knees and thighs. After half a mile it becomes (I am not exaggerating) an unbearable agony. You begin to wonder whether you will ever get to the end—still more, how on earth you are going to get back. Your pace grows slower and slower. You come to a stretch of a couple of hundred yards where it is all exceptionally low and you have to work yourself along in a squatting position. Then suddenly the roof opens out to a mysterious height—scene of an old fall of rock, probably—and for twenty whole yards you can stand upright. The relief is overwhelming. But after this there is another low stretch of a hundred yards and then a succession of beams which you have to crawl under. You go down on all fours; even this is a relief after the squatting business. But when you come to the end of the beams and try to get up again, you find that your knees have temporarily struck work and refuse to lift you. You call a halt, ignominiously, and say that you would like to rest for a minute or two. Your guide (a miner) is sympathetic. He knows that your muscles are not the same as his. " Only another four hundred yards," he says encouragingly; you feel that he might as well say another four hundred miles. But finally you do somehow creep as far as the coal face. You have gone a mile and taken the best part of an hour; a miner would do it in not much more than twenty minutes. Having got there, you have to sprawl in the coal dust and get your strength back for several minutes before you can even watch the work in progress with any kind of intelligence.

Coming back is worse than going, not only because you are already tired out but because the journey back to the shaft is probably slightly up hill. You get through the low places at the speed of a tortoise, and you have no shame now about calling a halt when your knees give way. Even the lamp you are carrying becomes a nuisance and probably when you stumble you drop it; whereupon, if it is a Davy lamp, it goes out. Ducking the beams becomes more and more of an effort, and sometimes you forget to duck. You try walking head down as the miners do, and then you bang your backbone. Even the miners bang their backbones fairly often. This is the reason why in very hot mines, where it is necessary to go about half naked, most of the miners have what they call " buttons down the back "—that is, a permanent scab on each vertebra. When the track is down hill the miners sometimes fit their clogs, which are hollow underneath, on to the trolley rails and slide down. In mines where the " travelling " is very bad all the miners carry sticks about two and a half feet long, hollowed out below the handle. In normal places you keep your hand on top of the stick and in the low places you slide your hand down into the hollow. These sticks are a great help, and the wooden crash-helmets—a comparatively recent invention—are a godsend. They look like a French or Italian steel helmet, but they are made of some kind of pith and very light, and so strong that you can take a violent blow on the head without feeling it. When finally you get back to the surface you have been perhaps three hours underground and travelled two miles, and you are more exhausted than you would be by a twenty-five-mile walk above ground. For a week afterwards your thighs are so stiff that coming downstairs is quite a difficult feat; you have to work your way down in a peculiar sidelong manner, without bending the knees. Your miner friends notice the stiffness of your walk and chaff you about it. (" How'd ta like to work down pit, eh ? " etc.) Yet even a miner who has been long away from work—from illness, for instance—when he comes back to the pit, suffers badly for the first few days.

It may seem that I am exaggerating, though no one
who has been down an old-fashioned pit (most of the
pits in England are old-fashioned) and actually gone as
far as the coal face, is likely to say so. But what I want
to emphasise is this. Here is this frightful business of
crawling to and fro, which to any normal person is a
hard day's work in itself; and it is not part of the miner's
work at all, it is merely an extra, like the City man's
daily ride in the Tube. The miner does that journey to
and fro, and sandwiched in between there are seven
and a half hours of savage work. I have never travelled
much more than a mile to the coal face; but often it is
three miles, in which case I and most people other than
coal-miners would never get there at all. This is the kind
of point that one is always liable to miss. When you
think of a coal-mine you think of depth, heat, darkness,
blackened figures hacking at walls of coal; you don't
think, necessarily, of those miles of creeping to and fro.
There is the question of time, also. A miner's working
shift of seven and a half hours does not sound very long,
but one has got to add on to it at least an hour a day for
" travelling," more often two hours and sometimes three.
Of course, the " travelling " is not technically work and
the miner is not paid for it; but it is as like work as
makes no difference. It is easy to say that miners don't
mind all this. Certainly, it is not the same for them as it
would be for you or me. They have done it since childhood, they have the right muscles hardened, and they
can move to and fro underground with a startling and
rather horrible agility. A miner puts his head down and
runs, with a long swinging stride, through places where
I can only stagger. At the workings you see them on all
fours, skipping round the pit props almost like dogs.
But it is quite a mistake to think that they enjoy it. I

have talked about this to scores of miners and they all admit that the " travelling " is hard work; in any case when you hear them discussing a pit among themselves the " travelling " is always one of the things they discuss. It is said that a shift always returns from work faster than it goes; nevertheless the miners all say that it is the coming away, after a hard day's work, that is especially irksome. It is part of their work and they are equal to it, but certainly it is an effort. It is comparable, perhaps, to climbing a smallish mountain before and after your day's work.

When you have been down two or three pits you begin to get some grasp of the processes that are going on underground. (I ought to say, by the way, that I know nothing whatever about the technical side of mining: I am merely describing what I have seen.) Coal lies in thin seams between enormous layers of rock, so that essentially the process of getting it out is like scooping the central layer from a Neapolitan ice. In the old days the miners used to cut straight into the coal with pick and crowbar—a very slow job because coal, when lying in its virgin state, is almost as hard as rock. Nowadays the preliminary work is done by an electrically-driven coal-cutter, which in principle is an immensely tough and powerful band-saw, running horizontally instead of vertically, with teeth a couple of inches long and half an inch or an inch thick. It can move backwards or forwards on its own power, and the men operating it can rotate it this way and that. Incidentally it makes one of the most awful noises I have ever heard, and sends forth clouds of coal dust which make it impossible to see more than two or three feet and almost impossible to breathe. The machine travels along the coal face cutting into the base of the coal and undermining it to the depth of five feet or five feet and a half; after this it is comparatively easy to extract the coal to the depth to which it has been undermined. Where it is " difficult getting," however, it has also to be loosened with explosives. A man with an electric drill, like a rather smaller version of the drills used in street-mending, bores holes at intervals in the coal, inserts blasting powder, plugs it with clay, goes round the corner if there is one handy (he is supposed to retire to twenty-five yards distance) and touches off the charge with an electric current. This is not intended to bring the coal out, only to loosen it. Occasionally, of course, the charge is too powerful, and then it not only brings the coal out but brings the roof down as well.

After the blasting has been done the " fillers " can tumble the coal out, break it up and shovel it on to the conveyor belt. It comes out at first in monstrous boulders which may weigh anything up to twenty tons. The conveyor belt shoots it on to tubs, and the tubs are shoved into the main road and hitched on to an endlessly revolving steel cable which drags them to the cage. Then they are hoisted, and at the surface the coal is sorted by being run over screens, and if necessary is washed as well. As far as possible the " dirt "—the shale, that is—is used for making the roads below. All that cannot be used is sent to the surface and dumped; hence the monstrous " dirt-heaps," like hideous grey mountains, which are the characteristic scenery of the coal areas. When the coal has been extracted to the depth to which the machine has cut, the coal face has advanced by five feet. Fresh props are put in to hold up the newly exposed roof, and during the next shift the conveyor belt is taken to pieces, moved five feet forward and re-assembled. As far as possible the three operations of cutting, blasting and extraction are done in three separate shifts, the cutting in the afternoon, the blasting at night (there is a law, not always kept, that forbids its being done when there are other men working near by), and the " filling " in the morning shift, which lasts from six in the morning until half past one.

Even when you watch the process of coal-extraction you probably only watch it for a short time, and it is not until you begin making a few calculations that you realise what a stupendous task the " fillers " are performing. Normally each man has to clear a space four or five yards wide. The cutter has undermined the coal to the depth of five feet, so that if the seam of coal is three or four feet high, each man has to cut out, break up and load on to the belt something between seven and twelve cubic yards of coal. This is to say, taking a cubic yard as weighing twenty-seven hundredweight, that each man is shifting coal at a speed approaching two tons an hour. I have just enough experience of pick and shovel work to be able to grasp what this means. When I am digging trenches in my garden, if I shift two tons of earth during the afternoon, I feel that I have earned my tea. But earth is tractable stuff compared with coal, and I don't have to work kneeling down, a thousand feet underground, in suffocating heat and swallowing coal dust with every breath I take; nor do I have to walk a mile bent double before I begin. The miner's job would be as much beyond my power as it would be to perform on the flying trapeze or to win the Grand National. I am not a manual labourer and please God I never shall be one, but there are some kinds of manual work that I could do if I had to. At a pitch I could be a tolerable road-sweeper or an inefficient gardener or even a tenth-rate farm hand. But by no conceivable amount of effort or training could I become a coal-miner; the work would kill me in a few weeks.

Watching coal-miners at work, you realise momentarily what different universes different people inhabit. Down there where coal is dug it is a sort of world apart which one can quite easily go through life without ever hearing about. Probably a majority of people would even prefer not to hear about it. Yet it is the absolutely necessary counterpart of our world above. Practically everything we do, from eating an ice to crossing the Atlantic, and from baking a loaf to writing a novel, involves the use of coal, directly or indirectly. For all the arts of peace coal is needed; if war breaks out it is needed all the more. In time of revolution the miner must go on working or the revolution must stop, for revolution as much as reaction needs coal. Whatever may be happening on the surface, the hacking and shovelling have got to continue without a pause, or at any rate without pausing for more than a few weeks at the most. In order that Hitler may march the goose-step, that the Pope may denounce Bolshevism, that the cricket crowds may assemble at Lord's, that the Nancy poets may scratch one another's backs, coal has got to be forthcoming. But on the whole we are not aware of it; we all know that we " must have coal," but we seldom or never remember what coal-getting involves. Here am I, sitting writing in front of my comfortable coal fire. It is April but I still need a fire. Once a fortnight the coal cart drives up to the door and men in leather jerkins carry the coal indoors in stout sacks smelling of tar and shoot it clanking into the coal-hole under the stairs. It is only very rarely, when I make a definite mental effort, that I connect this coal with that far-off labour in the mines. It is just " coal "—

something that I have got to have; black stuff that arrives mysteriously from nowhere in particular, like manna except that you have to pay for it. You could quite easily drive a car right across the north of England and never once remember that hundreds of feet below the road you are on the miners are hacking at the coal. Yet in a sense it is the miners who are driving your car forward. Their lamp-lit world down there is as necessary to the daylight world above as the root is to the flower.

It is not long since conditions in the mines were worse than they are now. There are still living a few very old women who in their youth have worked underground, with a harness round their waists and a chain that passed between their legs, crawling on all fours and dragging tubs of coal. They used to go on doing this even when they were pregnant. And even now, if coal could not be produced without pregnant women dragging it to and fro, I fancy we should let them do it rather than deprive ourselves of coal. But most of the time, of course, we should prefer to forget that they were doing it. It is so with all types of manual work; it keeps us alive, and we are oblivious of its existence. More than anyone else, perhaps, the miner can stand as the type of the manual worker, not only because his work is so exaggeratedly awful, but also because it is so vitally necessary and yet so remote from our experience, so invisible, as it were, that we are capable of forgetting it as we forget the blood in our veins. In a way it is even humiliating to watch coal-miners working. It raises in you a momentary doubt about your own status as an " intellectual " and a superior person generally. For it is brought home to you, at least while you are watching, that it is only because miners sweat their guts out that superior persons can remain superior. You and I and the editor of the *Times Lit. Supp.*, and the Nancy poets and the Archbishop of Canterbury and Comrade X, author of *Marxism for Infants*—all of us *really* owe the comparative decency of our lives to poor drudges underground, blackened to the eyes, with their throats full of coal dust, driving their shovels forward with arms and belly muscles of steel.

CHAPTER III

WHEN THE MINER comes up from the pit his face is
so pale that it is noticeable even through the mask of
coal dust. This is due to the foul air that he has been
breathing, and will wear off presently. To a Southerner,
new to the mining districts, the spectacle of a shift of
several hundred miners streaming out of the pit is
strange and slightly sinister. Their exhausted faces,
with the grime clinging in all the hollows, have a fierce,
wild look. At other times, when their faces are clean,
there is not much to distinguish them from the rest of
the population. They have a very upright square-
shouldered walk, a reaction from the constant bending
underground, but most of them are shortish men and
their thick ill-fitting clothes hide the splendour of their
bodies. The most definitely distinctive thing about them
is the blue scars on their noses. Every miner has blue
scars on his nose and forehead, and will carry them to
his death. The coal dust of which the air underground
is full enters every cut, and then the skin grows over it
and forms a blue stain like tattooing, which in fact it is.
Some of the older men have their foreheads veined like
Roquefort cheeses from this cause.

As soon as the miner comes above ground he gargles
a little water to get the worst of the coal dust out of his
throat and nostrils, and then goes home and either
washes or does not wash according to his temperament.
From what I have seen I should say that a majority

of miners prefer to eat their meal first and wash afterwards, as I should do in their circumstances. It is the
normal thing to see a miner sitting down to his tea with
a Christy-minstrel face, completely black except for
very red lips which become clean by eating. After his
meal he takes a largish basin of water and washes very
methodically, first his hands, then his chest, neck and
armpits, then his forearms, then his face and scalp (it
is on the scalp that the grime clings thickest), and then
his wife takes the flannel and washes his back. He has
only washed the top half of his body and probably his
navel is still a nest of coal dust, but even so it takes some
skill to get passably clean in a single basin of water.
For my own part I found I needed two complete baths
after going down a coal-mine. Getting the dirt out of
one's eyelids is a ten minutes' job in itself.

At some of the larger and better appointed collieries
there are pithead baths. This is an enormous advantage,
for not only can the miner wash himself all over every
day, in comfort and even luxury, but at the baths he
has two lockers where he can keep his pit clothes separate
from his day clothes, so that within twenty minutes of
emerging as black as a negro he can be riding off to a
football match dressed up to the nines. But it is only
comparatively few mines that have baths, partly because
a seam of coal does not last for ever, so that it is not
necessarily worth building a bath every time a shaft is
sunk. I cannot get hold of exact figures, but it seems
likely that rather less than one miner in three has access
to a pithead bath. Probably a large majority of miners
are completely black from the waist down for at least
six days a week. It is almost impossible for them to
wash all over in their own homes. Every drop of water
has got to be heated up, and in a tiny living-room which

contains, apart from the kitchen range and a quantity
of furniture, a wife, some children and probably a dog,
there is simply not room to have a proper bath. Even
with a basin one is bound to splash the furniture. Middle-
class people are fond of saying that the miners would
not wash themselves properly even if they could, but
this is nonsense, as is shown by the fact that where pithead baths exist practically all the men use them. Only
among the very old men does the belief still linger that
washing one's legs " causes lumbago." Moreover the
pithead baths, where they exist, are paid for wholly or
partly by the miners themselves, out of the Miners'
Welfare Fund. Sometimes the colliery company sub-
scribes, sometimes the Fund bears the whole cost.
But doubtless even at this late date the old ladies in
Brighton boarding-houses are saying that " if you
give those miners baths they only use them to keep
coal in."

As a matter of fact it is surprising that miners wash as
regularly as they do, seeing how little time they have
between work and sleep. It is a great mistake to think of
a miner's working day as being only seven and a half
hours. Seven and a half hours is the time spent actually
on the job, but, as I have already explained, one has got
to add on to this time taken up in " travelling," which
is seldom less than an hour and may often be three hours.
In addition most miners have to spend a considerable
time in getting to and from the pit. Throughout the
industrial districts there is acute shortage of houses, and
it is only in the small mining villages, where the village
is grouped round the pit, that the men can be certain of
living near their work. In the larger mining towns where
I have stayed, nearly everyone went to work by bus;
half-a-crown a week seemed to be the normal amount to

spend on fares. One miner I stayed with was working on the morning shift, which was from six in the morning till half-past one. He had to be out of bed at a quarter to four and got back somewhere after three in the afternoon. In another house where I stayed a boy of fifteen was working on the night shift. He left for work at nine at night and got back at eight in the morning, had his breakfast and then promptly went to bed and slept till six in the evening; so that his leisure time amounted to about four hours a day—actually a good deal less, if you take off the time for washing, eating and dressing.

The adjustments a miner's family have to make when he is changed from one shift to another must be tiresome in the extreme. If he is on the night shift he gets home in time for breakfast, on the morning shift he gets home in the middle of the afternoon, and on the afternoon shift he gets home in the middle of the night; and in each case, of course, he wants his principal meal of the day as soon as he returns. I notice that the Rev. W. R. Inge, in his book *England*, accuses the miners of gluttony. From my own observation I should say that they eat astonishingly little. Most of the miners I stayed with ate slightly less than I did. Many of them declare that they cannot do their day's work if they have had a heavy meal beforehand, and the food they take with them is only a snack, usually bread-and-dripping and cold tea. They carry it in a flat tin called a snap-can which they strap to their belts. When a miner gets back late at night his wife waits up for him, but when he is on the morning shift it seems to be the custom for him to get his breakfast for himself. Apparently the old superstition that it is bad luck to see a woman before going to work on the morning shift is not quite extinct. In the old days, it is said, a

miner who happened to meet a woman in the early
morning would often turn back and do no work that
day.

Before I had been in the coal areas I shared the widespread illusion that miners are comparatively well paid.
One hears it loosely stated that a miner is paid ten or
eleven shillings a shift, and one does a small multiplica-
tion sum and concludes that every miner is earning
round about £3 a week or £150 a year. But the state-
ment that a miner receives ten or eleven shillings a shift
is very misleading. To begin with, it is only the actual
coal " getter " who is paid at this rate; a " dataller," for
instance, who attends to the roofing, is paid at a lower
rate, usually eight or nine shillings a shift. Again, when
the coal " getter " is paid piecework, so much per ton
extracted, as is the case in many mines, he is dependent
on the quality of the coal; a breakdown in the machinery
or a " fault "—that is, a streak of rock running through
the coal seam—may rob him of his earnings for a day or
two at a time. But in any case one ought not to think of
the miner as working six days a week, fifty-two weeks a
year. Almost certainly there will be a number of days
when he is " laid off." The average earning per shift
worked for every mine-worker, of all ages and both sexes,
in Great Britain in 1934, was 9s. 1¾d.[1] If everyone were
in work all the time, this would mean that the mine-
worker was earning a little over £142 a year, or nearly
£2 15s. a week. His real income, however, is far lower
than this, for the 9s. 1¾d. is merely an average calcula-
tion on shifts actually worked and takes no account of
blank days.

I have before me five pay-checks belonging to a Yorkshire miner, for five weeks (not consecutive) at the

[1] From the *Colliery Year Book and Coal Trades Directory* for 1935.

beginning of 1936. Averaging them up, the gross weekly
wage they represent is £2 15s. 2d.; this is an average of
nearly 9s. 2½d. a shift. But these pay-checks are for the
winter, when nearly all mines are running full time.
As spring advances the coal trade slacks off and more and
more men are " temporarily stopped," while others still
technically in work are laid off for a day or two in every
week. It is obvious therefore that £150 or even £142 is an
immense over-estimate for the mine-worker's yearly
income. As a matter of fact, for the year 1934 the average
gross earnings of all miners throughout Great Britain
was only £115 11s. 6d. It varied considerably from
district to district, rising as high as £133 2s. 8d. in Scotland, while in Durham it was a little under £105 or
barely more than £2 a week. I take these figures from
The Coal Scuttle, by Mr. Joseph Jones, Mayor of Barnsley,
Yorkshire. Mr. Jones adds:

" These figures cover the earnings of youths as well as
adults and of the higher as well as the lower-paid grades . . .
any particularly high earning would be included in these
figures, as would the earnings of certain officials and other
higher-paid men as well as the higher amounts paid for
overtime work. . . .

" *The figures, being averages, fail . . . to reveal the position of
thousands of adult workers whose earnings were substantially below the
average and who received only 30s. to 40s. or less per week.*"

Mr. Jones's italics. But please notice that even these
wretched earnings are *gross* earnings. On top of this there
are all kinds of stoppages which are deducted from the
miner's wages every week. Here is a list of weekly stoppages which was given me as typical in one Lancashire
district:

						s.	*d.*
Insurance (unemployment and health).						1	5
Hire of lamp	.	.	.	.	.		6
For sharpening tools		.	.	.			6
Check-weighman	.	.	.	.			9
Infirmary	.	.	.	.	.		2
Hospital .	.	.	.	.	.		1
Benevolent Fund	.	.	.	.			6
Union fees	.	.	.	.	.		6
Total				.	.	4	5

Some of these stoppages, such as the Benevolent Fund and the union fees, are, so to speak, the miner's own responsibility, others are imposed by the colliery company. They are not the same in all districts. For instance, the iniquitous swindle of making the miner pay for the hire of his lamp (at sixpence a week he buys the lamp several times over in a single year) does not obtain everywhere. But the stoppages always seem to total up to about the same amount. On the Yorkshire miner's five pay-checks, the average gross earning per week is £2 15s. 2d.; the average net earning, after the stoppages have come off, is only £2 11s. 4d.—a reduction of 3s. 10d. a week. But the pay-check, naturally, only mentions stoppages which are imposed by or paid through the colliery company; one has got to add the union fees, bringing the total reduction up to something over four shillings. Probably it is safe to say that stoppages of one kind and another cut four shillings or thereabouts from *every* adult miner's weekly wage. So that the £115 11s. 6d. which was the mine-worker's average earning throughout Great Britain in 1934 should really be something nearer £105. As against this, most miners receive allowances in kind, being able to purchase coal for their own use at a reduced rate, usually eight or nine shillings a ton. But according to Mr. Jones, quoted above, " the average value of all allowances in kind for the country as a whole is only fourpence a day." And this fourpence a day is offset, in many cases, by the amount the miner has to spend on fares in getting to and from the pit. So, taking the industry as a whole, the sum the miner can actually bring home and call his own does not average more, perhaps slightly less, than two pounds a week.

Meanwhile, how much coal is the average miner producing?

The tonnage of coal raised yearly per person employed in mining rises steadily though rather slowly. In 1914 every mine-worker produced, on an average, 253 tons of coal; in 1934 he produced 280 tons.[1] This of course is an average figure for mine-workers of all kinds; those actually working at the coal face extract an enormously greater amount—in many cases, probably, well over a thousand tons each. But taking 280 tons as a representative figure, it is worth noticing what a vast achievement this is. One gets the best idea of it by comparing a miner's lifework with somebody else's. If I live to be sixty I shall probably have produced thirty novels, or enough to fill two medium-sized library shelves. In the same period the average miner produces 8,400 tons of coal; enough coal to pave Trafalgar Square nearly two feet deep or to supply seven large families with fuel for over a hundred years.

Of the five pay-checks I mentioned above, no less than three are rubber-stamped with the words " death stoppage." When a miner is killed at work it is usual for the other miners to make up a subscription, generally of

[1] *The Coal Scuttle*. The *Colliery Year Book and Coal Trades Directory* gives a slightly higher figure.

a shilling each, for his widow, and this is collected by the colliery company and automatically deducted from their wages. The significant detail here is the *rubber stamp*. The rate of accidents among miners is so high, compared with that in other trades, that casualties are taken for granted almost as they would be in a minor war. Every year one miner in about nine hundred is killed and one in about six is injured; most of these injuries, of course, are petty ones, but a fair number amount to total disablement. This means that if a miner's working life is forty years the chances are nearly seven to one against his escaping injury and not much more than twenty to one against his being killed outright. No other trade approaches this in dangerousness; the next most dangerous is the shipping trade, one sailor in a little under 1,300 being killed every year. The figures I have given apply, of course, to mine-workers as a whole; for those actually working underground the proportion of injuries would be very much higher. Every miner of long standing that I have talked to had either been in a fairly serious accident himself or had seen some of his mates killed, and in every mining family they tell you tales of fathers, brothers or uncles killed at work. (" And he fell seven hundred feet, and they wouldn't never have collected t'pieces only he were wearing a new suit of oilskins," etc., etc., etc.) Some of these tales are appalling in the extreme. One miner, for instance, described to me how a mate of his, a " dataller," was buried by a fall of rock. They rushed to him and managed to uncover his head and shoulders so that he could breathe, and he was alive and spoke to them. Then they saw that the roof was coming down again and had to run to save themselves; the " dataller " was buried a second time. Once again they rushed to him and got his head and shoulders free, and again he was alive and spoke to them. Then the roof came down a third time, and this time they could not uncover him for several hours, after which, of course, he was dead. But the miner who told me the story (he had been buried himself on one occasion, but he was lucky enough to have his head jammed between his legs so that there was a small space in which he could breathe) did not think it was a particularly appalling one. Its significance, for him, was that the " dataller " had known perfectly well that the place where he was working was unsafe, and had gone there in daily expectation of an accident. " And it worked on his mind to that extent that he got to kissing his wife before he went to work. And she told me afterwards that it were over twenty year since he'd kissed her."

The most obviously understandable cause of accidents is explosions of gas, which is always more or less present in the atmosphere of the pit. There is a special lamp which is used to test the air for gas, and when it is present in at all large quantities it can be detected by the flame of an ordinary Davy lamp burning blue. If the wick can be turned up to its full extent and the flame is still blue, the proportion of gas is dangerously high; it is, nevertheless, difficult to detect, because it does not distribute itself evenly throughout the atmosphere but hangs about in cracks and crevices. Before starting work a miner often tests for gas by poking his lamp into all the corners. The gas may be touched off by a spark during blasting operations, or by a pick striking a spark from a stone, or by a defective lamp, or by " gob fires "—spontaneously generated fires which smoulder in the coal dust and are very hard to put out. The great mining disasters which happen from time to time, in which several hundred men are killed, are usually caused by explosions; hence one tends to think of explosions as the chief danger of mining. Actually, the great majority of accidents are due to the normal every-day dangers of the pit; in particular, to falls of roof. There are, for instance, " pot-holes "— circular holes from which a lump of stone big enough to kill a man shoots out with the promptitude of a bullet. With, so far as I can remember, only one exception, all the miners I have talked to declared that the new machinery, and " speeding up " generally, has made the work more dangerous. This may be partly due to conservatism, but they can give plenty of reasons. To begin with, the speed at which the coal is now extracted means that for hours at a time a dangerously large stretch of roof remains unpropped. Then there is the vibration, which tends to shake everything loose, and the noise, which makes it harder to detect signs of danger. One must remember that a miner's safety underground depends largely on his own care and skill. An experienced miner claims to know by a sort of instinct when the roof is unsafe; the way he puts it is that he "can feel the weight on him." He can, for instance, hear the faint creaking of the props. The reason why wooden props are still generally preferred to iron girders is that a wooden prop which is about to collapse gives warning by creaking, whereas a girder flies out unexpectedly. The devastating noise of the machines makes it impossible to hear anything else, and thus the danger is increased.

When a miner is hurt it is of course impossible to attend to him immediately. He lies crushed under several hundredweight of stone in some dreadful cranny underground, and even after he has been extricated it is necessary to drag his body a mile or more, perhaps, through galleries where nobody can stand upright.

Usually when you talk to a man who has been injured you find that it was a couple of hours or so before they got him to the surface. Sometimes, of course, there are accidents to the cage. The cage is shooting several hundred yards up or down at the speed of an express train, and it is operated by somebody on the surface who cannot see what is happening. He has very delicate indicators to tell him how far the cage has got, but it is possible for him to make a mistake, and there have been cases of the cage crashing into the pit-bottom at its very maximum speed. This seems to me a dreadful way to die. For as that tiny steel box whizzes through the blackness there must come a moment when the ten men who are locked inside it *know* that something has gone wrong; and the remaining seconds before they are smashed to pieces hardly bear thinking about. A miner told me he was once in a cage in which something went wrong. It did not slow up when it should have done, and they thought the cable must have snapped. As it happened they got to the bottom safely, but when he stepped out he found that he had broken a tooth; he had been clenching his teeth so hard in expectation of that frightful crash.

Apart from accidents miners seem to be healthy, as obviously they have got to be, considering the muscular efforts demanded of them. They are liable to rheumatism and a man with defective lungs does not last long in that dust-impregnated air, but the most characteristic industrial disease is nystagmus. This is a disease of the eyes which makes the eyeballs oscillate in a strange manner when they come near a light. It is due presumably to working in half-darkness, and sometimes results in total blindness. Miners who are disabled in this way or any other way are compensated by the colliery company, sometimes with a lump sum, sometimes with a weekly pension. This pension never amounts to more than twenty-nine shillings a week; if it falls below fifteen shillings the disabled man can also get something from the dole or the P.A.C. If I were a disabled miner I should very much prefer the lump sum, for then at any rate I should know that I had got my money. Disability pensions are not guaranteed by any centralised fund, so that if the colliery company goes bankrupt that is the end of the disabled miner's pension, though he does figure among the other creditors.

In Wigan I stayed for a while with a miner who was suffering from nystagmus. He could see across the room but not much further. He had been drawing compensation of twenty-nine shillings a week for the past nine months, but the colliery company were now talking of putting him on " partial compensation " of fourteen shillings a week. It all depended on whether the doctor passed him as fit for light work " on top." Even if the doctor did pass him there would, needless to say, be no light work available, but he could draw the dole and the company would have saved itself fifteen shillings a week. Watching this man go to the colliery to draw his compensation, I was struck by the profound differences that are still made by *status*. Here was a man who had been half blinded in one of the most useful of all jobs and was drawing a pension to which he had a perfect right, if anybody has a right to anything. Yet he could not, so to speak, *demand* this pension—he could not, for instance, draw it when and how he wanted it. He had to go to the colliery once a week at a time named by the company, and when he got there he was kept waiting about for hours in the cold wind. For all I know he was also expected to touch his cap and show gratitude to whomever paid him; at any rate he had to waste an afternoon and spend sixpence in bus fares. It is very different for a member of the bourgeoisie, even such a down-at-heel member as I am. Even when I am on the verge of starvation I have certain rights attaching to my bourgeois status. I do not earn much more than a miner earns, but I do at least get it paid into my bank in a gentlemanly manner and can draw it out when I choose. And even when my account is exhausted the bank people are still passably polite.

This business of petty inconvenience and indignity, of being kept waiting about, of having to do everything at other people's convenience, is inherent in working-class life. A thousand influences constantly press a working man down into a *passive* rôle. He does not act, he is acted upon. He feels himself the slave of mysterious authority and has a firm conviction that " they " will never allow him to do this, that and the other. Once when I was hop-picking I asked the sweated pickers (they earn something under sixpence an hour) why they did not form a union. I was told immediately that " they " would never allow it. Who were " they " ? I asked. Nobody seemed to know; but evidently " they " were omnipotent.

A person of bourgeois origin goes through life with some expectation of getting what he wants, within reasonable limits. Hence the fact that in times of stress " educated " people tend to come to the front; they are no more gifted than the others and their " education " is generally quite useless in itself, but they are accustomed to a certain amount of deference and consequently have the cheek necessary to a commander. That they *will* come to the front seems to be taken for granted, always and everywhere. In Lissagaray's *History of the Commune* there is an interesting passage describing the shootings that took place after the Commune had been suppressed. The authorities were shooting the ringleaders, and as they did not know who the ringleaders were, they were picking them out on the principle that those of better class would be the ringleaders. An officer walked down a line of prisoners, picking out likely-looking types. One man was shot because he was wearing a watch, another because he " had an intelligent face." I should not like to be shot for having an intelligent face, but I do agree that in almost any revolt the leaders would tend to be people who could pronounce their aitches.

CHAPTER IV

As you walk through the industrial towns you lose yourself in labyrinths of little brick houses blackened by smoke, festering in planless chaos round miry alleys and little cindered yards where there are stinking dust-bins and lines of grimy washing and half-ruinous w.c.'s. The interiors of these houses are always very much the same, though the number of rooms varies between two and five. All have an almost exactly similar living-room, ten or fifteen feet square, with an open kitchen range; in the larger ones there is a scullery as well, in the smaller ones the sink and copper are in the living-room. At the back there is the yard, or part of a yard shared by a number of houses, just big enough for the dustbin and the w.c. Not a single one has hot water laid on. You might walk, I suppose, through literally hundreds of miles of streets inhabited by miners, every one of whom, when he is in work, gets black from head to foot every day, without ever passing a house in which one could have a bath. It would have been very simple to install a hot-water system working from the kitchen range, but the builder saved perhaps ten pounds on each house by not doing so, and at the time when these houses were built no one imagined that miners wanted baths.

For it is to be noted that the majority of these houses are old, fifty or sixty years old at least, and great numbers of them are by any ordinary standard not fit for human habitation. They go on being tenanted simply because there are no others to be had. And that is the central fact about housing in the industrial areas : not that the houses are poky and ugly, and insanitary and comfortless, or that they are distributed in incredibly filthy slums round belching foundries and stinking canals and slag-heaps that deluge them with sulphurous smoke—though all this is perfectly true—but simply that there are not enough houses to go round.

" Housing shortage " is a phrase that has been bandied about pretty freely since the war, but it means very little to anyone with an income of more than £10 a week, or even £5 a week for that matter. Where rents are high the difficulty is not to find houses but to find tenants. Walk down any street in Mayfair and you will see " To Let " boards in half the windows. But in the industrial areas the mere difficulty of getting hold of a house is one of the worst aggravations of poverty. It means that people will put up with anything—any hole and corner slum, any misery of bugs and rotting floors and cracking walls, any extortion of skinflint landlords and black-mailing agents—simply to get a roof over their heads. I have been into appalling houses, houses in which I would not live a week if you paid me, and found that the tenants had been there twenty and thirty years and only hoped they might have the luck to die there. In general these conditions are taken as a matter of course, though not always. Some people hardly seem to realise that such things as decent houses exist and look on bugs and leaking roofs as acts of God; others rail bitterly against their landlords; but all cling desperately to their houses lest worse should befall. So long as the housing shortage continues the local authorities cannot do much to make existing houses more livable. They can " condemn " a house, but they cannot order it to be pulled down till the tenant has another house to go to; and so the condemned houses remain standing and are all the worse for being condemned, because naturally the landlord will not spend more than he can help on a house which is going to be demolished sooner or later. In a town like Wigan, for instance, there are over two thousand houses standing which have been condemned for years, and whole sections of the town would be condemned *en bloc* if there were any hope of other houses being built to replace them. Towns like Leeds and Sheffield have scores of thousands of " back to back " houses which are all of a condemned type but will remain standing for decades.

I have inspected great numbers of houses in various mining towns and villages and made notes on their essential points. I think I can best give an idea of what conditions are like by transcribing a few extracts from my notebook, taken more or less at random. They are only brief notes and they will need certain explanations which I will give afterwards. Here are a few from Wigan:

1. House in Wallgate quarter. Blind back type. One up, one down. Living-room measures 12 ft. by 10 ft., room upstairs the same. Alcove under stairs measuring 5 ft. by 5 ft. and serving as larder, scullery and coal hole. Windows will open. Distance to lavatory 50 yards. Rent 4s. 9d., rates 2s. 6d., total 7s. 3d.

2. Another near by. Measurements as above, but no alcove under stairs, merely a recess two feet deep containing the sink— no room for larder, etc. Rent 3s. 2d., rates 2s., total 5s. 2d.

3. Another as above but with no alcove at all, merely sink in living-room just inside front door. Rent 3s. 9d., rates 3s., total 6s. 9d.

4. House in Scholes quarter. Condemned house. One up, one down. Rooms 15 ft. by 15 ft. Sink and copper in living-room, coal hole under stairs. Floor subsiding. No windows will

open. House decently dry. Landlord good. Rent 3s. 8d., rates
2s. 6d., total 6s. 2d.

5. Another near by. Two up, two down and coal hole. Walls
falling absolutely to pieces. Water comes into upstairs rooms
in quantities. Floor lopsided. Downstairs windows will not
open. Landlord bad. Rent 6s., rates 3s. 6d., total 9s. 6d.

6. House in Greenough's Row. One up, two down. Living-
room 13 ft. by 8 ft. Walls coming apart and water comes in.
Back windows will not open, front ones will. Ten in family
with eight children very near together in age. Corporation are
trying to evict them for overcrowding but cannot find another
house to send them to. Landlord bad. Rent 4s., rates 2s. 3d.,
total 6s. 3d.

So much for Wigan. I have pages more of the same
type. Here is one from Sheffield—a typical specimen of
Sheffield's several score thousand " back to back "
houses:

House in Thomas Street. Back to back, two up, one down
(i.e. a three-storey house with one room on each storey).
Cellar below. Living-room 14 ft. by 10 ft., and rooms above
corresponding. Sink in living-room. Top floor has no door
but gives on open stairs. Walls in living-room slightly damp,
walls in top rooms coming to pieces and oozing damp on all
sides. House is so dark that light has to be kept burning all
day. Electricity estimated at 6d. a day (probably an exaggeration). Six in family, parents and four children. Husband (on
P.A.C.) is tuberculous. One child in hospital, the others appear
healthy. Tenants have been seven years in this house. Would
move, but no other house available. Rent 6s. 6d., rates included.

Here are one or two from Barnsley:

1. House in Wortley Street. Two up, one down. Living-room
12 ft. by 10 ft. Sink and copper in living-room, coal hole under
stairs. Sink worn almost flat and constantly overflowing. Walls
not too sound. Penny in slot, gas-light. House very dark and
gas-light estimated at 4d. a day. Upstairs rooms are really one

large room partitioned into two. Walls very bad—wall of back room cracked right through. Window-frames coming to pieces and have to be stuffed with wood. Rain comes through in several places. Sewer runs under house and stinks in summer but Corporation " says they can't do nowt." Six people in house, two adults and four children, the eldest aged fifteen. Youngest but one attending hospital—tuberculosis suspected. House infested by bugs. Rent 5s. 3d., including rates.

2. House in Peel Street. Back to back, two up, two down and large cellar. Living-room 10 ft. square with copper and sink. The other downstairs room the same size, probably intended as parlour but used as bedroom. Upstairs rooms the same size as those below. Living-room very dark. Gas-light estimated at 4½d. a day. Distance to lavatory 70 yards. Four beds in house for eight people—two old parents, two adult girls (the eldest aged twenty-seven), one young man and three children. Parents have one bed, eldest son another, and remaining five people share the other two. Bugs very bad—" You can't keep 'em down when it's 'ot." Indescribable squalor in downstairs room and smell upstairs almost unbearable. Rent 5s. 7½d., including rates.

3. House in Mapplewell (small mining village near Barnsley). Two up, one down. Living-room 14 ft. by 12 ft. Sink in living-room. Plaster cracking and coming off walls. No shelves in oven. Gas leaking slightly. The upstairs rooms each 10 ft. by 8 ft. Four beds (for six persons, all adult), but " one bed does nowt," presumably for lack of bedclothes. Room nearest stairs has no door and stairs have no banister, so that when you step out of bed your foot hangs in vacancy and you may fall ten feet on to stones. Dry rot so bad that one can see through the floor into the room below. Bugs, but " I keeps 'em down with sheep dip." Earth road past these cottages is like a muck-heap and said to be almost impassable in winter. Stone lavatories at ends of garden in semi-ruinous condition. Tenants have been twenty-two years in this house. Are £11 in arrears with rent, and have been paying an extra 1s. a week to pay this off. Landlord now refuses this and has served orders to quit. Rent 5s., including rates.

And so on and so on and so on. I could multiply examples by the score—they could be multiplied by the hundred thousand if anyone chose to make a house to house inspection throughout the industrial districts. Meanwhile some of the expressions I have used need explaining. " One up, one down " means one room on each storey—i.e. a two-roomed house. " Back to back " houses are two houses built in one, each side of the house being somebody's front door, so that if you walk down a row of what is apparently twelve houses you are in reality seeing not twelve houses but twenty-four. The front houses give on the street and the back ones on the yard, and there is only one way out of each house. The effect of this is obvious. The lavatories are in the yard at the back, so that if you live on the side facing the street, to get to the lavatory or the dust-bin you have to go out of the front door and walk round the end of the block—a distance that may be as much as two hundred yards; if you live at the back, on the other hand, your outlook is on to a row of lavatories. There are also houses of what is called the " blind back " type, which are single houses, but in which the builder has omitted to put in a back door—from pure spite, apparently. The windows which refuse to open are a peculiarity of old mining towns. Some of these towns are so undermined by ancient workings that the ground is constantly sub- siding and the houses above slip sideways. In Wigan you pass whole rows of houses which have slid to startling angles, their windows being ten or twenty degrees out of the horizontal. Sometimes the front wall bellies out- ward till it looks as though the house were seven months gone in pregnancy. It can be refaced, but the new facing soon begins to bulge again. When a house sinks at all suddenly its windows are jammed for ever and the door has to be refitted. This excites no surprise locally. The story of the miner who comes home from work and finds that he can only get indoors by smashing down the front door with an axe is considered humorous. In some cases I have noted " Landlord good " or " Landlord bad," because there is great variation in what the slum-dwellers say about their landlords. I found—one might expect it, perhaps—that the small landlords are usually the worst. It goes against the grain to say this, but one can see why it should be so. Ideally, the worst type of slum landlord is a fat wicked man, preferably a bishop, who is drawing an immense income from extortionate rents. Actually, it is a poor old woman who has invested her life's savings in three slum houses, inhabits one of them and tries to live on the rent of the other two—never, in consequence, having any money for repairs.

But mere notes like these are only valuable as re-minders to myself. To me as I read them they bring back what I have seen, but they cannot in themselves give much idea of what conditions are like in those fearful northern slums. Words are such feeble things. What is the use of a brief phrase like " roof leaks " or " four beds for eight people " ? It is the kind of thing your eye slides over, registering nothing. And yet what a wealth of misery it can cover ! Take the question of overcrowding, for instance. Quite often you have eight or even ten people living in a three-roomed house. One of these rooms is a living-room, and as it probably measures about a dozen feet square and contains, besides the kitchen range and the sink, a table, some chairs and a dresser, there is no room in it for a bed. So there are eight or ten people sleeping in two small rooms, probably in at most four beds. If some of these people are adults and have to go to work, so much the worse.

In one house, I remember, three grown-up girls shared the same bed and all went to work at different hours, each disturbing the others when she got up or came in; in another house a young miner working on the night shift slept by day in a narrow bed in which another member of the family slept by night. There is an added difficulty when there are grown-up children, in that you cannot let adolescent youths and girls sleep in the same bed. In one family I visited there were a father and mother and a son and daughter aged round about seventeen, and only two beds for the lot of them. The father slept with the son and the mother with the daughter; it was the only arrangement that ruled out the danger of incest. Then there is the misery of leaking roofs and oozing walls, which in winter makes some rooms almost uninhabitable. Then there are bugs. Once bugs get into a house they are in it till the crack of doom; there is no sure way of exterminating them. Then there are the windows that will not open. I need not point out what this must mean, in summer, in a tiny stuffy living-room where the fire, on which all the cooking is done, has to be kept burning more or less constantly. And there are the special miseries attendant upon back to back houses. A fifty yards' walk to the lavatory or the dust-bin is not exactly an inducement to be clean. In the front houses—at any rate in a side-street where the Corporation don't interfere—the women get into the habit of throwing their refuse out of the front door, so that the gutter is always littered with tea-leaves and bread crusts. And it is worth considering what it is like for a child to grow up in one of the back alleys where its gaze is bounded by a row of lavatories and a wall.

In such places as these a woman is only a poor drudge muddling among an infinity of jobs. She may keep up her spirits, but she cannot keep up her standards of cleanliness and tidiness. There is always something to be done, and no conveniences and almost literally not room to turn round. No sooner have you washed one child's face than another's is dirty; before you have washed the crocks from one meal the next is due to be cooked. I found great variation in the houses I visited. Some were as decent as one could possibly expect in the circumstances, some were so appalling that I have no hope of describing them adequately. To begin with, the smell, the dominant and essential thing, is indescribable. But the squalor and the confusion ! A tub full of filthy water here, a basin full of unwashed crocks there, more crocks piled in any odd corner, torn newspaper littered everywhere, and in the middle always the same dreadful table covered with sticky oilcloth and crowded with cooking pots and irons and half-darned stockings and pieces of stale bread and bits of cheese wrapped round with greasy newspaper ! And the congestion in a tiny room where getting from one side to the other is a complicated voyage between pieces of furniture, with a line of damp washing getting you in the face every time you move and the children as thick underfoot as toadstools ! There are scenes that stand out vividly in my memory. The almost bare living-room of a cottage in a little mining village, where the whole family was out of work and everyone seemed to be underfed; and the big family of grown-up sons and daughters sprawling aimlessly about, all strangely alike with red hair, splendid bones and pinched faces ruined by malnutrition and idleness; and one tall son sitting by the fireplace, too listless even to notice the entry of a stranger, and slowly peeling a sticky sock from a bare foot. A dreadful room in Wigan where all the furniture seemed to be made of packing cases and barrel staves and was coming to pieces at that; and an old woman with a blackened neck and her hair coming down denouncing her landlord in a Lancashire-Irish accent; and her mother, aged well over ninety, sitting in the background on the barrel that served her as a commode and regarding us blankly with a yellow, cretinous face. I could fill up pages with memories of similar interiors.

Of course the squalor of these people's houses is sometimes their own fault. Even if you live in a back to back house and have four children and a total income of thirty-two and sixpence a week from the P.A.C., there is no *need* to have unemptied chamber-pots standing about in your living-room. But it is equally certain that their circumstances do not encourage self-respect. The determining factor is probably the number of children. The best-kept interiors I saw were always childless houses or houses where there were only one or two children; with, say, six children in a three-roomed house it is quite impossible to keep anything decent. One thing that is very noticeable is that the worst squalors are never downstairs. You might visit quite a number of houses, even among the poorest of the unemployed, and bring away a wrong impression. These people, you might reflect, cannot be so badly off if they still have a fair amount of furniture and crockery. But it is in the rooms upstairs that the gauntness of poverty really discloses itself. Whether this is because pride makes people cling to their living-room furniture to the last, or because bedding is more pawnable, I do not know, but certainly many of the bedrooms I saw were fearful places. Among people who have been unemployed for several years continuously I should say it is the exception to have anything like a full set of bedclothes. Often there is nothing that can be properly called bedclothes at all—just a heap of old overcoats and miscellaneous rags on a rusty iron bedstead. In this way overcrowding is aggravated. One family of four persons that I knew, a father and mother and two children, possessed two beds but could only use one of them because they had not enough bedding for the other.

Anyone who wants to see the effects of the housing shortage at their very worst should visit the dreadful caravan-dwellings that exist in numbers in many of the northern towns. Ever since the war, in the complete impossibility of getting houses, parts of the population have overflowed into supposedly temporary quarters in fixed caravans. Wigan, for instance, with a population of about 85,000, has round about 200 caravan-dwellings with a family in each—perhaps somewhere near 1,000 people in all. How many of these caravan-colonies exist throughout the industrial areas it would be difficult to discover with any accuracy. The local authorities are reticent about them and the census report of 1931 seems to have decided to ignore them. But so far as I can discover by enquiry they are to be found in most of the larger towns in Lancashire and Yorkshire, and perhaps further north as well. The probability is that throughout the north of England there are some thousands, perhaps tens of thousands of *families* (not individuals) who have no home except a fixed caravan.

But the word " caravan " is very misleading. It calls up a picture of a cosy gypsy-encampment (in fine weather, of course) with wood fires crackling and children picking blackberries and many-coloured washing fluttering on the lines. The caravan-colonies in Wigan and Sheffield are not like that. I had a look at several of them, I inspected those in Wigan with considerable care, and I have never seen comparable squalor except in the Far East. Indeed when I saw them I was immediately reminded of the filthy kennels in which I have seen Indian coolies living in Burma. But, as a matter of fact, nothing in the East could ever be quite as bad, for in the East you haven't our clammy, penetrating cold to contend with, and the sun is a disinfectant.

Along the banks of Wigan's miry canal are patches of waste ground on which the caravans have been dumped like rubbish shot out of a bucket. Some of them are actually gypsy caravans, but very old ones and in bad repair. The majority are old single-decker buses (the rather smaller buses of ten years ago) which have been taken off their wheels and propped up with struts of wood. Some are simply wagons with semi-circular slats on top, over which canvas is stretched, so that the people inside have nothing but canvas between them and the outer air. Inside, these places are usually about five feet wide by six high (I could not stand quite upright in any of them) and anything from six to fifteen feet long. Some, I suppose, are inhabited by only one person, but I did not see any that held less than two persons, and some of them contained large families. One, for instance, measuring fourteen feet long, had seven people in it—seven people in about 450 cubic feet of space; which is to say that each person had for his entire dwelling a space *a good deal* smaller than one compartment of a public lavatory. The dirt and congestion of these places is such that you cannot well imagine it unless you have tested it with your own eyes and more particularly your nose. Each contains a tiny cottage kitchener and such furniture as can be crammed in—sometimes two beds, more usually one, into which the whole family have to huddle as best they can. It is almost impossible to sleep on the floor, because the damp soaks up from below. I was shown mattresses which were still wringing wet at eleven in the morning. In winter it is so cold that the kitcheners have to be kept burning day and night, and the windows, needless to say, are never opened. Water is got from a hydrant common to the whole colony, some of the caravan-dwellers having to walk 150 or 200 yards for every bucket of water. There are no sanitary arrangements at all. Most of the people construct a little hut to serve as a lavatory on the tiny patch of ground surrounding their caravan, and once a week dig a deep hole in which to bury the refuse. All the people I saw in these places, especially the children, were unspeakably dirty, and I do not doubt that they were lousy as well. They could not possibly be otherwise. The thought that haunted me as I went from caravan to caravan was, What can happen in those cramped interiors when anybody dies? But that, of course, is the kind of question you hardly care to ask.

Some of the people have been in their caravans for many years. Theoretically the Corporation are doing away with the caravan-colonies and getting the inhabitants out into houses; but as the houses don't get built, the caravans remain standing. Most of the people I talked to had given up the idea of ever getting a decent habitation again. They were all out of work, and a job and a house seemed to them about equally remote and impossible. Some hardly seemed to care; others realised quite clearly in what misery they were living. One woman's face stays by me, a worn skull-like face on which was a look of intolerable misery and degradation. I gathered that in that dreadful pigsty, struggling to keep her large brood of children clean, she felt as I should feel if I were coated all over with dung. One must remember that these people are not gypsies; they are decent English people who have all, except the children born there, had homes of their own in their day; besides, their caravans are greatly inferior to those of gypsies and they have not the great advantage of being on the move. No doubt there are still middle-class people who think that the Lower Orders don't mind that kind of thing and who, if they happened to pass a caravan-colony in the train, would immediately assume that the people lived there from choice. I never argue nowadays with that kind of person. But it is worth noticing that the caravan-dwellers don't even save money by living there, for they are paying about the same rents as they would for houses. I could not hear of any rent lower than five shillings a week (five shillings for 200 cubic feet of space!) and there are even cases where the rent is as high as ten shillings. Somebody must be making a good thing out of those caravans! But clearly their continued existence is due to the housing shortage and not directly to poverty.

Talking once with a miner I asked him when the housing shortage first became acute in his district; he answered, " When we were told about it," meaning that till recently people's standards were so low that they took almost any degree of overcrowding for granted. He added that when he was a child his family had slept eleven in a room and thought nothing of it, and that later, when he was grown-up, he and his wife had lived in one of the old-style back to back houses in which you not only had to walk a couple of hundred yards to the lavatory but often had to wait in a queue when you got there, the lavatory being shared by thirty-six people. And when his wife was sick with the illness that killed her, she still had to make that two hundred yards' journey to the lavatory. This, he said, was the kind of

thing people would put up with " till they were told
about it."

I do not know whether this is true. What is certain is
that nobody *now* thinks it bearable to sleep eleven in a
room, and that even people with comfortable incomes
are vaguely troubled by the thought of " the slums."
Hence the clatter about " rehousing " and " slum
clearance " which we have had at intervals ever since
the war. Bishops, politicians, philanthropists and what
not enjoy talking piously about " slum clearance,"
because they can thus divert attention from more serious
evils and pretend that if you abolish the slums you
abolish poverty. But all this talk has led to surprisingly
small results. So far as one can discover, the congestion
is no better, perhaps slightly worse, than it was a dozen
years ago. There is certainly great variation in the speed
at which the different towns are attacking their housing
problem. In some towns building seems to be almost at
a standstill, in others it is proceeding rapidly and the
private landlord is being driven out of business. Liverpool, for instance, has been very largely rebuilt, mainly
by the efforts of the Corporation. Sheffield, too, is being
torn down and rebuilt pretty fast, though perhaps, considering the unparalleled beastliness of its slums, not
quite fast enough.[1]

Why rehousing has on the whole moved so slowly, and
why some towns can borrow money for building purposes so much more easily than others, I do not know.
Those questions would have to be answered by someone
who knows more about the machinery of local government than I do. A Corporation house costs normally
somewhere between three and four hundred pounds; it

[1] The number of Corporation houses in process of construction in Sheffield at
the beginning of 1936 was 1,398. To replace the slum areas entirely Sheffield is said
to need 100,000 houses.

costs rather less when it is built by " direct labour " than when built by contract. The rent of these houses would average something over twenty pounds a year not counting rates, so one would think that, even allowing for overhead expenses and interest on loans, it would pay any Corporation to build as many houses as could be tenanted. In many cases, of course, the houses would have to be inhabited by people on the P.A.C., so that the local bodies would merely be taking money out of one pocket and putting it into another—i.e. paying out money in the form of relief and taking it back in the form of rent. But they have got to pay the relief in any case, and at present a proportion of what they pay is being swallowed up by private landlords. The reasons given for the slow rate of building are lack of money and the difficulty of getting hold of sites—for Corporation houses are not erected piecemeal but in " estates," sometimes of hundreds of houses at a time. One thing that always strikes me as mysterious is that so many of the northern towns see fit to build themselves immense and luxurious public buildings at the same time as they are in crying need of dwelling houses. The town of Barnsley, for instance, recently spent close on £150,000 on a new town hall, although admittedly needing at least 2,000 new working-class houses, not to mention public baths. (The public baths in Barnsley contain *nineteen* men's slipper baths—this in a town of 70,000 inhabitants, largely miners, not one of whom has a bath in his house !) For £150,000 it could have built 350 Corporation houses and still had £10,000 to spend on a town hall. However, as I say, I do not pretend to understand the mysteries of local government. I merely record the fact that houses are desperately needed and are being built, on the whole, with paralytic slowness.

Still, houses *are* being built, and the Corporation building estates, with their row upon row of little red houses,
all much liker than two peas (where did that expression
come from ? Peas have great individuality) are a regular
feature of the outskirts of the industrial towns. As to
what they are like and how they compare with the slum
houses, I can best give an idea by transcribing two more
extracts from my diary. The tenants' opinions of their
houses vary greatly, so I will give one favourable extract
and one unfavourable. Both of these are from Wigan and
both are the cheaper " non-parlour type " houses:

1. House in Beech Hill Estate.
Downstairs. Large living-room with kitchener fireplace, cup-
boards and fixed dresser, composition floor. Small hallway,
largish kitchen. Up to date electric cooker hired from Corporation at much the same rate as a gas cooker.
Upstairs. Two largish bedrooms, one tiny one—suitable only
for a boxroom or temporary bedroom. Bathroom, w.c., with
hot and cold water.
Smallish garden. These vary throughout the estate, but
mostly rather smaller than an allotment.
Four in family, parents and two children. Husband in good
employ. Houses appear well built and are quite agreeable to
look at. Various restrictions, e.g. it is forbidden to keep poultry
or pigeons, take in lodgers, sublet or start any kind of business
without leave from the Corporation. (This is easily granted in
the case of taking in lodgers, but not in any of the others.)
Tenant very well satisfied with house and proud of it. Houses
in this estate all well kept. Corporation are good about repairs,
but keep tenants up to the mark with regard to keeping the
place tidy, etc.
Rent 11*s*. 3*d*., including rates. Bus fare into town 2*d*.

2. House in Welly Estate.
Downstairs. Living-room 14 ft. by 10 ft., kitchen a good

deal smaller, tiny larder under stairs, small but fairly good bathroom. Gas cooker, electric lighting. Outdoor w.c.

Upstairs. One bedroom 12 ft. by 10 ft. with tiny fireplace, another the same size without fireplace, another 7 ft. by 6 ft. Best bedroom has small wardrobe let into wall.

Garden about 20 yards by 10.

Six in family, parents and four children, eldest son nineteen, eldest daughter twenty-two. None in work except eldest son. Tenants very discontented. Their complaints are: " House is cold, draughty and damp. Fireplace in living-room gives out no heat and makes room very dusty—attributed to its being set too low. Fireplace in best bedroom too small to be of any use. Walls upstairs cracking. Owing to uselessness of tiny bedroom, 5 are sleeping in one bedroom, 1 (the eldest son) in the other."

Gardens in this estate all neglected.

Rent 10s. 3d., inclusive. Distance to town a little over a mile—there is no bus here.

I could multiply examples, but these two are enough, as the types of Corporation houses being built do not vary greatly from place to place. Two things are immediately obvious. The first is that at their very worst the Corporation houses are better than the slums they replace. The mere possession of a bathroom and a bit of garden would outweigh almost any disadvantage. The other is that they are much more expensive to live in. It is common enough for a man to be turned out of a condemned house where he is paying six or seven shillings a week and given a Corporation house where he has to pay ten. This only affects those who are in work or have recently been in work, because when a man is on the P.A.C. his rent is assessed at a quarter of his dole, and if it is more than this he gets an extra allowance; in any case, there are certain classes of Corporation houses to which people on the dole are not admitted. But there are other ways in which life in a Corporation estate is expensive, whether you are in work or out of it. To begin with, owing to the higher rents, the shops in the estate are much more expensive and there are not so many of them. Then again, in a comparatively large, detached house, away from the frowsy huddle of the slum, it is much colder and more fuel has to be burnt. And again there is the expense, especially for a man in work, of getting to and from town. This last is one of the more obvious problems of rehousing. Slum clearance means diffusion of the population. When you rebuild on a large scale, what you do in effect is to scoop out the centre of the town and redistribute it on the outskirts. This is all very well in a way; you have got the people out of fetid alleys into places where they have room to breathe; but from the point of view of the people themselves, what you have done is to pick them up and dump them down five miles from their work. The simplest solution is flats. If people are going to live in large towns at all they must learn to live on top of one another. But the northern working people do not take kindly to flats; even where flats exist they are contemptuously named " tenements." Almost everyone will tell you that he " wants a house of his own," and apparently a house in the middle of an unbroken block of houses a hundred yards long seems to them more " their own " than a flat situated in mid-air.

To revert to the second of the two Corporation houses I have just mentioned. The tenant complained that the house was cold, damp, and so forth. Perhaps the house was jerry-built, but equally probably he was exaggerating. He had come there from a filthy hovel in the middle of Wigan which I happened to have inspected previously; while there he had made every effort to get hold of a Corporation house, and he was no sooner in the Corporation house than he wanted to be back in the slum. This looks like mere captiousness but it covers a perfectly genuine grievance. In very many cases, perhaps in half the cases, I found that the people in Corporation houses don't really like them. They are glad to get out of the stink of the slum, they know that it is better for their children to have space to play about in, but they don't feel really at home. The exceptions are usually people in good employ who can afford to spend a little extra on fuel and furniture and journeys, and who in any case are of " superior " type. The others, the typical slum-dwellers, miss the frowsy warmth of the slum. They complain that " out in the country," i.e. on the edge of the town, they are " starving " (freezing). Certainly most Corporation estates are pretty bleak in winter. Some I have been through, perched on treeless clayey hillsides and swept by icy winds, would be horrible places to live in. It is not that slum-dwellers want dirt and congestion for their own sakes, as the fat-bellied bourgeoisie love to believe. (See for instance the conversation about slum-clearance in Galsworthy's *Swan Song*, where the rentier's cherished belief that the slum-dweller makes the slum, and not vice versa, is put into the mouth of a philanthropic Jew.) Give people a decent house and they will soon learn to keep it decent. Moreover, with a smart-looking house to live up to they improve in self-respect and cleanliness, and their children start life with better chances. Nevertheless, in a Corporation estate there is an uncomfortable, almost prison-like atmosphere, and the people who live there are perfectly well aware of it.

And it is here that one comes on the central difficulty

of the housing problem. When you walk through the smoke-dim slums of Manchester you think that nothing is needed except to tear down these abominations and build decent houses in their place. But the trouble is that in destroying the slum you destroy other things as well. Houses are desperately needed and are not being built fast enough; but in so far as rehousing is being done, it is being done—perhaps it is unavoidable—in a monstrously inhuman manner. I don't mean merely that the houses are new and ugly. All houses have got to be new at some time, and as a matter of fact the type of Corporation house now being built is not at all offensive to look at. On the outskirts of Liverpool there are what amount to whole towns consisting entirely of Corporation houses, and they are quite pleasing to the eye; the blocks of workers' flats in the centre of the town, modelled, I believe, on the workers' flats in Vienna, are definitely fine buildings. But there is something ruthless and soulless about the whole business. Take, for instance, the restrictions with which you are burdened in a Corporation house. You are not allowed to keep your house and garden as you want them— in some estates there is even a regulation that every garden must have the same kind of hedge. You are not allowed to keep poultry or pigeons. The Yorkshire miners are fond of keeping homer pigeons; they keep them in the back yard and take them out and race them on Sundays. But pigeons are messy birds and the Corporation suppresses them as a matter of course. The restrictions about shops are more serious. The number of shops in a Corporation estate is rigidly limited, and it is said that preference is given to the Co-op. and the chain stores; this may not be strictly true, but certainly those are the shops that one usually sees there. This is bad enough for the general public, but from the point of view of the independent shopkeeper it is a disaster. Many a small shopkeeper is utterly ruined by some rehousing scheme which takes no notice of his existence. A whole section of the town is condemned *en bloc*; presently the houses are pulled down and the people are transferred to some housing estate miles away. In this way all the small shopkeepers of the quarter have their whole clientele taken away from them at a single swoop and receive not a penny of compensation. They cannot transfer their business to the estate, because even if they can afford the move and the much higher rents, they would probably be refused a licence. As for pubs, they are banished from the housing estates almost completely, and the few that remain are dismal sham-Tudor places fitted out by the big brewery companies and very expensive. For a middle-class population this would be a nuisance—it might mean walking a mile to get a glass of beer; for a working-class population, which uses the pub as a kind of club, it is a serious blow at communal life. It is a great achievement to get slum-dwellers into decent houses, but it is unfortunate that, owing to the peculiar temper of our time, it is also considered necessary to rob them of the last vestiges of their liberty. The people themselves feel this, and it is this feeling that they are rationalising when they complain that their new houses—so much better, *as* houses, than those they have come out of—are cold and uncomfortable and " unhomelike."

I sometimes think that the price of liberty is not so much eternal vigilance as eternal dirt. There are some Corporation estates in which new tenants are systematic-ally deloused before being allowed into their houses. All their possessions except what they stand up in are taken away from them, fumigated and sent on to the new house. This procedure has its points, for it *is* a pity that people should take bugs into brand new houses (a bug will follow you about in your luggage if he gets half a chance), but it is the kind of thing that makes you wish that the word " hygiene " could be dropped out of the dictionary. Bugs are bad, but a state of affairs in which men will allow themselves to be dipped like sheep is worse. Perhaps, however, when it is a case of slum clearance, one must take for granted a certain amount of restrictions and inhumanity. When all is said and done, the most important thing is that people shall live in decent houses and not in pigsties. I have seen too much of slums to go into Chestertonian raptures about them. A place where the children can breathe clean air, and women have a few conveniences to save them from drudgery, and a man has a bit of garden to dig in, *must* be better than the stinking backstreets of Leeds and Sheffield. On balance, the Corporation Estates are better than the slums; but only by a small margin.

When I was looking into the housing question I visited and inspected numbers of houses, perhaps a hundred or two hundred houses altogether, in various mining towns and villages. I cannot end this chapter without remarking on the extraordinary courtesy and good nature with which I was received everywhere. I did not go alone— I always had some local friend among the unemployed to show me round—but even so, it is an impertinence to go poking into strangers' houses and asking to see the cracks in the bedroom wall. Yet everyone was astonishingly patient and seemed to understand almost without explanation why I was questioning them and what I wanted to see. If any unauthorised person walked into *my* house and began asking me whether the roof leaked and whether I was much troubled by bugs and what I thought of my landlord, I should probably tell him to go to hell. This only happened to me once, and in that case the woman was slightly deaf and took me for a Means Test nark; but even she relented after a while and gave me the information I wanted.

I am told that it is bad form for a writer to quote his own reviews, but I want here to contradict a reviewer in the *Manchester Guardian* who says apropos of one of my books:

" Set down in Wigan or Whitechapel Mr. Orwell would still exercise an unerring power of closing his vision to all that is good in order to proceed with his wholehearted vilification of humanity."

Wrong. Mr. Orwell was " set down " in Wigan for quite a while and it did not inspire him with any wish to vilify humanity. He liked Wigan very much—the people, not the scenery. Indeed, he has only one fault to find with it, and that is in respect of the celebrated Wigan Pier, which he had set his heart on seeing. Alas ! Wigan Pier has been demolished, and even the spot where it used to stand is no longer certain.

CHAPTER V

WHEN you see the unemployment figures quoted at two millions, it is fatally easy to take this as meaning that two million people are out of work and the rest of the population is comparatively comfortable. I admit that till recently I was in the habit of doing so myself. I used to calculate that if you put the registered unemployed at round about two millions and threw in the destitute and those who for one reason and another were not registered, you might take the number of underfed people in England (for *everyone* on the dole or thereabouts is underfed) as being, at the very most, five millions.

This is an enormous under-estimate, because, in the first place, the only people shown on unemployment figures are those actually drawing the dole—that is, in general, heads of families. An unemployed man's dependants do not figure on the list unless they too are drawing a separate allowance. A Labour Exchange officer told me that to get at the real number of people *living on* (not drawing) the dole, you have got to multiply the official figures by something over three. This alone brings the number of unemployed to round about six millions. But in addition there are great numbers of people who are in work but who, from a financial point of view, might equally well be unemployed, because they are not drawing anything that can be described as a living wage.[1] Allow for these and their dependants, throw in as before the old-age pensioners, the destitute and other nondescripts, and you get an *underfed* population of well over ten millions. Sir John Orr puts it at twenty millions.

Take the figures for Wigan, which is typical enough of the industrial and mining districts. The number of insured workers is round about 36,000 (26,000 men and 10,000 women). Of these, the number unemployed at the beginning of 1936 was about 10,000. But this was in winter when the mines are working full time; in summer it would probably be 12,000. Multiply by three, as above, and you get 30,000 or 36,000. The total population of Wigan is a little under 87,000; so that at any moment more than one person in three out of the whole population—not merely the registered workers—is either drawing or living on the dole. Those ten or twelve thousand unemployed contain a steady core of from four to five thousand miners who have been continuously unemployed for the past seven years. And Wigan is not especially badly off as industrial towns go. Even in Sheffield, which has been doing well for the last year or so because of wars and rumours of war, the proportion of unemployment is about the same—one in three of registered workers unemployed.

When a man is first unemployed, until his insurance stamps are exhausted, he draws " full benefit," of which the rates are as follows:

	per week
Single man	17s.
Wife	9s.
Each child below 14 . . .	3s.

[1] For instance, a recent census of the Lancashire cotton mills revealed the fact that over 40,000 *full-time* employees receive less than thirty shillings a week each. In Preston, to take only one town, the number receiving *over* thirty shillings a week was 640 and the number receiving *under* thirty shillings was 3,113.

Thus in a typical family of parents and three children of whom one was over 14, the total income would be 32s. per week, plus anything that might be earned by the eldest child. When a man's stamps are exhausted, before being turned over to the P.A.C. (Public Assistance Committee), he receives twenty-six weeks' " transitional benefit " from the U.A.B. (Unemployment Assistance Board), the rates being as follows:

	per week
Single man	15s.
Man and wife	24s.
Children, 14–18	6s.
Children, 11–14	4s. 6d.
Children, 8–11	4s.
Children, 5–8	3s. 6d.
Children, 3–5	3s

Thus on the U.A.B. the income of the typical family of five persons would be 37s. 6d. a week if no child was in work. When a man is on the U.A.B. a quarter of his dole is regarded as rent, with a minimum of 7s. 6d. a week. If the rent he is paying is more than a quarter of his dole he receives an extra allowance, but if it is less than 7s. 6d., a corresponding amount is deducted. Payments on the P.A.C. theoretically come out of the local rates, but are backed by a central fund. The rates of benefit are:

	per week
Single man	12s. 6d.
Man and wife	23s.
Eldest child	4s.
Any other child	3s.

Being at the discretion of the local bodies these rates vary slightly, and a single man may or may not get an extra 2s. 6d. weekly, bringing his benefit up to 15s. As

on the U.A.B., a quarter of a married man's dole is
regarded as rent. Thus in the typical family considered
above the total income would be 33s. a week, a quarter
of this being regarded as rent. In addition, in most
districts a coal allowance of 1s. 6d. a week (1s. 6d. is
equivalent to about a hundredweight of coal) is granted
for six weeks before and six weeks after Christmas.

It will be seen that the income of a family on the dole
normally averages round about thirty shillings a week.
One can write at least a quarter of this off as rent, which
is to say that the average person, child or adult, has got
to be fed, clothed, warmed, and otherwise cared-for for
six or seven shillings a week. Enormous groups of people,
probably at least a third of the whole population of the
industrial areas, are living at this level. The Means Test
is very strictly enforced, and you are liable to be refused
relief at the slightest hint that you are getting money
from another source. Dock-labourers, for instance, who
are generally hired by the half day, have to sign on at a
Labour Exchange twice daily; if they fail to do so it is
assumed that they have been working and their dole is
reduced correspondingly. I have seen cases of evasion of
the Means Test, but I should say that in the industrial
towns, where there is still a certain amount of communal
life and everyone has neighbours who know him, it is
much harder than it would be in London. The usual
method is for a young man who is actually living with
his parents to get an accommodation address, so that
supposedly he has a separate establishment and draws a
separate allowance. But there is much spying and tale-
bearing. One man I knew, for instance, was seen feeding
his neighbour's chickens while the neighbour was away.
It was reported to the authorities that he " had a job
feeding chickens " and he had great difficulty in refuting

this. The favourite joke in Wigan was about a man who was refused relief on the ground that he " had a job carting firewood." He had been seen, it was said, carting firewood at night. He had to explain that he was not carting firewood but doing a moonlight flit. The " firewood " was his furniture.

The most cruel and evil effect of the Means Test is the way in which it breaks up families. Old people, sometimes bedridden, are driven out of their homes by it. An old age pensioner, for instance, if a widower, would normally live with one or other of his children; his weekly ten shillings goes towards the household expenses, and probably he is not badly cared for. Under the Means Test, however, he counts as a " lodger " and if he stays at home his children's dole will be docked. So, perhaps at seventy or seventy-five years of age, he has to turn out into lodgings, handing his pension over to the lodging-house keeper and existing on the verge of starvation. I have seen several cases of this myself. It is happening all over England at this moment, thanks to the Means Test.

Nevertheless, in spite of the frightful extent of unemployment, it is a fact that poverty—extreme poverty—is less in evidence in the industrial North than it is in London. Everything is poorer and shabbier, there are fewer motor-cars and fewer well-dressed people; but also there are fewer people who are obviously destitute. Even in a town the size of Liverpool or Manchester you are struck by the fewness of the beggars. London is a sort of whirlpool which draws derelict people towards it, and it is so vast that life there is solitary and anonymous. Until you break the law nobody will take any notice of you, and you can go to pieces as you could not possibly do in a place where you had neighbours who knew you.

But in the industrial towns the old communal way of life has not yet broken up, tradition is still strong and almost everyone has a family—potentially, therefore, a home. In a town of 50,000 or 100,000 inhabitants there is no casual and as it were unaccounted-for population; nobody sleeping in the streets, for instance. Moreover, there is just this to be said for the unemployment regulations, that they do not discourage people from marrying. A man and wife on twenty-three shillings a week are not far from the starvation line, but they can make a home of sorts; they are vastly better off than a single man on fifteen shillings. The life of a single unemployed man is dreadful. He lives sometimes in a common lodging-house, more often in a " furnished " room for which he usually pays six shillings a week, finding himself as best he can on the other nine (say six shillings a week for food and three for clothes, tobacco and amusements). Of course he cannot feed or look after himself properly, and a man who pays six shillings a week for his room is not encouraged to be indoors more than is necessary. So he spends his days loafing in the public library or any other place where he can keep warm. That—keeping warm—is almost the sole preoccupation of a single unemployed man in winter. In Wigan a favourite refuge was the pictures, which are fantastically cheap there. You can always get a seat for fourpence, and at the matinee at some houses you can even get a seat for twopence. Even people on the verge of starvation will readily pay twopence to get out of the ghastly cold of a winter afternoon. In Sheffield I was taken to a public hall to listen to a lecture by a clergyman, and it was by a long way the silliest and worst-delivered lecture I have ever heard or ever expect to hear. I found it physically impossible to sit it out; indeed my feet carried me out, seemingly of their own accord, before it was half way through. Yet the hall was thronged with unemployed men; they would have sat through far worse drivel for the sake of a warm place to shelter in.

At times I have seen unmarried men on the dole living in the extreme of misery. In one town I remember a whole colony of them who were squatting, more or less illicitly, in a derelict house which was practically falling down. They had collected a few scraps of furniture, presumably off refuse-tips, and I remember that their sole table was an old marble-topped wash-hand-stand. But this kind of thing is exceptional. A working-class bachelor is a rarity, and so long as a man is married unemployment makes comparatively little alteration in his way of life. His home is impoverished but it is still a home, and it is noticeable everywhere that the anomalous position created by unemployment—the man being out of work while the woman's work continues as before—has not altered the relative status of the sexes. In a working-class home it is the man who is the master and not, as in a middle-class home, the woman or the baby. Practically never, for instance, in a working-class home, will you see the man doing a stroke of the housework. Unemployment has not changed this convention, which on the face of it seems a little unfair. The man is idle from morning to night but the woman is as busy as ever—more so, indeed, because she has to manage with less money. Yet so far as my experience goes the women do not protest. I believe that they, as well as the men, feel that a man would lose his manhood if, merely because he was out of work, he developed into a " Mary Ann."

But there is no doubt about the deadening, debilitating effect of unemployment upon everybody, married or

single, and upon men more than upon women. The best
intellects will not stand up against it. Once or twice it
has happened to me to meet unemployed men of genuine
literary ability; there are others whom I haven't met
but whose work I occasionally see in the magazines.
Now and again, at long intervals, these men will produce
an article or a short story which is quite obviously better
than most of the stuff that gets whooped up by the blurb-
reviewers. Why, then, do they make so little use of their
talents? They have all the leisure in the world; why
don't they sit down and write books? Because to write
books you need not only comfort and solitude—and
solitude is never easy to attain in a working-class home—
you also need peace of mind. You can't settle to anything, you can't command the spirit of *hope* in which
anything has got to be created, with that dull evil cloud
of unemployment hanging over you. Still, an unemployed
man who feels at home with books can at any rate
occupy himself by reading. But what about the man
who cannot read without discomfort? Take a miner,
for instance, who has worked in the pit since childhood
and has been trained to be a miner and nothing else.
How the devil is he to fill up the empty days? It is
absurd to say that he ought to be looking for work.
There is no work to look for, and everybody knows
it. You can't go on looking for work every day for seven
years. There are allotments, which occupy the time and
help to feed a family, but in a big town there are only
allotments for a small proportion of the people. Then
there are the occupational centres which were started a
few years ago to help the unemployed. On the whole
this movement has been a failure, but some of the centres
are still flourishing. I have visited one or two of them.
There are shelters where the men can keep warm and

there are periodical classes in carpentering, boot-making, leather-work, handloom-weaving, basket-work, sea-grass work, etc., etc.; the idea being that the men can make furniture and so forth, not for sale but for their own homes, getting tools free and materials cheaply. Most of the Socialists I have talked to denounce this movement as they denounce the project—it is always being talked about but it never comes to anything—to give the unemployed small-holdings. They say that the occupational centres are simply a device to keep the unemployed quiet and give them the illusion that something is being done for them. Undoubtedly that *is* the underlying motive. Keep a man busy mending boots and he is less likely to read the *Daily Worker*. Also there is a nasty Y.M.C.A. atmosphere about these places which you can feel as soon as you go in. The unemployed men who frequent them are mostly of the cap-touching type—the type who tells you oilily that he is " Temperance " and votes Conservative. Yet even here you feel yourself torn both ways. For probably it is better that a man should waste his time even with such rubbish as sea-grass work than that for years upon end he should do absolutely *nothing*.

By far the best work for the unemployed is being done by the N.U.W.M.—National Unemployed Workers' Movement. This is a revolutionary organisation intended to hold the unemployed together, stop them blacklegging during strikes and give them legal advice against the Means Test. It is a movement that has been built out of nothing by the pennies and efforts of the unemployed themselves. I have seen a good deal of the N.U.W.M., and I greatly admire the men, ragged and underfed like the others, who keep the organisation going. Still more I admire the tact and patience with which they do

it; for it is not easy to coax even a penny-a-week subscription out of the pockets of people on the P.A.C. As
I said earlier, the English working class do not show
much capacity for leadership, but they have a wonderful
talent for organisation. The whole trade union movement
testifies to this; so do the excellent working-men's clubs
—really a sort of glorified co-operative pub, and
splendidly organised—which are so common in Yorkshire. In many towns the N.U.W.M. have shelters and
arrange speeches by Communist speakers. But even at
these shelters the men who go there do nothing but sit
round the stove and occasionally play a game of
dominoes. If this movement could be combined with
something along the lines of the occupational centres,
it would be nearer what is needed. It is a deadly thing to
see a skilled man running to seed, year after year, in
utter, hopeless idleness. It ought not to be impossible to
give him the chance of using his hands and making
furniture and so forth for his own home, without turning
him into a Y.M.C.A. cocoa-drunkard. We may as well
face the fact that several million men in England will—
unless another war breaks out—never have a real job
this side the grave. One thing that probably could be
done and certainly ought to be done as a matter of
course, is to give every unemployed man a patch of
ground and free tools if he chose to apply for them. It is
disgraceful that men who are expected to keep alive on
the P.A.C. should not even have the chance to grow vegetables for their families.

To study unemployment and its effects you have got to
go to the industrial areas. In the South unemployment
exists, but it is scattered and queerly unobtrusive. There
are plenty of rural districts where a man out of work is
almost unheard-of, and you don't anywhere see the

spectacle of whole blocks of cities living on the dole and
the P.A.C. It is only when you lodge in streets where
nobody has a job, where getting a job seems about as
probable as owning an aeroplane and much *less* probable than winning fifty pounds in the Football Pool, that
you begin to grasp the changes that are being worked in
our civilisation. For a change *is* taking place, there is no
doubt about that. The attitude of the submerged working
class is profoundly different from what it was seven or
eight years ago.

I first became aware of the unemployment problem in
1928. At that time I had just come back from Burma,
where unemployment was only a word, and I had gone
to Burma when I was still a boy and the post-war boom
was not quite over. When I first saw unemployed men at
close quarters, the thing that horrified and amazed me
was to find that many of them were *ashamed* of being
unemployed. I was very ignorant, but not so ignorant
as to imagine that when the loss of foreign markets
pushes two million men out of work, those two million
are any more to blame than the people who draw
blanks in the Calcutta Sweep. But at that time nobody
cared to admit that unemployment was inevitable,
because this meant admitting that it would probably
continue. The middle classes were still talking about
" lazy idle loafers on the dole " and saying that " these
men could all find work if they wanted to," and naturally
these opinions percolated to the working class themselves.
I remember the shock of astonishment it gave me, when
I first mingled with tramps and beggars, to find that
a fair proportion, perhaps a quarter, of these beings
whom I had been taught to regard as cynical parasites,
were decent young miners and cotton-workers gazing at
their destiny with the same sort of dumb amazement

as an animal in a trap. They simply could not understand what was happening to them. They had been
brought up to work, and behold ! it seemed as if they
were never going to have the chance of working again.
In their circumstances it was inevitable, at first, that
they should be haunted by a feeling of personal degradation. That was the attitude towards unemployment in
those days : it was a disaster which happened to *you* as an
individual and for which *you* were to blame.

When a quarter of a million miners are unemployed, it
is part of the order of things that Alf Smith, a miner living
in the back streets of Newcastle, should be out of work.
Alf Smith is merely one of the quarter million, a statistical unit. But no human being finds it easy to regard
himself as a statistical unit. So long as Bert Jones across
the street is still at work, Alf Smith is bound to feel himself dishonoured and a failure. Hence that frightful
feeling of impotence and despair which is almost the
worst evil of unemployment—far worse than any hard-
ship, worse than the demoralisation of enforced idleness,
and only less bad than the physical degeneracy of Alf
Smith's children, born on the P.A.C. Everyone who saw
Greenwood's play *Love on the Dole* must remember that
dreadful moment when the poor, good, stupid working
man beats on the table and cries out, " O God, send me
some work ! " This was not dramatic exaggeration, it
was a touch from life. That cry must have been uttered,
in almost those words, in tens of thousands, perhaps
hundreds of thousands of English homes, during the past
fifteen years.

But, I think not again—or at least, not so often.
That is the real point : people are ceasing to kick against
the pricks. After all, even the middle classes—yes, even
the bridge clubs in the country towns—are beginning to

realise that there is such a thing as unemployment. The
" My dear, I don't *believe* in all this nonsense about unemployment. Why, only last week we wanted a man to
weed the garden, and we simply couldn't get one. They
don't *want* to work, that's all it is ! " which you heard
at every decent tea-table five years ago, is growing
perceptibly less frequent. As for the working class
themselves, they have gained immensely in economic
knowledge. I believe that the *Daily Worker* has accom-
plished a great deal here : its influence is out of all proportion to its circulation. But in any case they have had
their lesson well rubbed into them, not only because
unemployment is so widespread but because it has
lasted so long. When people live on the dole for years
at a time they grow used to it, and drawing the dole,
though it remains unpleasant, ceases to be shameful.
Thus the old, independent, workhouse-fearing tradition
is undermined, just as the ancient fear of debt is undermined by the hire-purchase system. In the back streets
of Wigan and Barnsley I saw every kind of privation,
but I probably saw much less *conscious* misery than I
should have seen ten years ago. The people have at any
rate grasped that unemployment is a thing they cannot
help. It is not only Alf Smith who is out of work now ;
Bert Jones is out of work as well, and both of them have
been " out " for years. It makes a great deal of difference
when things are the same for everybody.

So you have whole populations settling down, as it
were, to a lifetime on the P.A.C. And what I think is
admirable, perhaps even hopeful, is that they have
managed to do it without going spiritually to pieces.
A working man does not disintegrate under the strain
of poverty as a middle-class person does. Take, for instance, the fact that the working class think nothing

of getting married on the dole. It annoys the old ladies in Brighton, but it is a proof of their essential good sense; they realise that losing your job does not mean that you cease to be a human being. So that in one way things in the distressed areas are not so bad as they might be. Life is still fairly normal, more normal than one really has the right to expect. Families are impoverished, but the family-system has not broken up. The people are in effect living a reduced version of their former lives. Instead of raging against their destiny they have made things tolerable by lowering their standards.

But they don't necessarily lower their standards by cutting out luxuries and concentrating on necessities; more often it is the other way about—the more natural way, if you come to think of it. Hence the fact that in a decade of unparalleled depression, the consumption of all cheap luxuries has increased. The two things that have probably made the greatest difference of all are the movies and the mass-production of cheap smart clothes since the war. The youth who leaves school at fourteen and gets a blind-alley job is out of work at twenty, probably for life; but for two pounds ten on the hire-purchase system he can buy himself a suit which, for a little while and at a little distance, looks as though it had been tailored in Savile Row. The girl can look like a fashion plate at an even lower price. You may have three halfpence in your pocket and not a prospect in the world, and only the corner of a leaky bedroom to go home to; but in your new clothes you can stand on the street corner, indulging in a private daydream of yourself as Clark Gable or Greta Garbo, which compensates you for a great deal. And even at home there is generally a cup of tea going—a " nice cup of tea "— and Father, who has been out of work since 1929, is temporarily happy because he has a sure tip for the Cesarewitch.

Trade since the war has had to adjust itself to meet the demands of underpaid, underfed people, with the result that a luxury is nowadays almost always cheaper than a necessity. One pair of plain solid shoes costs as much as two ultra-smart pairs. For the price of one square meal you can get two pounds of cheap sweets. You can't get much meat for threepence, but you can get a lot of fish-and-chips. Milk costs threepence a pint and even "mild" beer costs fourpence, but aspirins are seven a penny and you can wring forty cups of tea out of a quarter-pound packet. And above all there is gambling, the cheapest of all luxuries. Even people on the verge of starvation can buy a few days' hope ("Something to live for," as they call it) by having a penny on a sweep-stake. Organised gambling has now risen almost to the status of a major industry. Consider, for instance, a phenomenon like the Football Pools, with a turnover of about six million pounds a year, almost all of it from the pockets of working-class people. I happened to be in Yorkshire when Hitler re-occupied the Rhineland. Hitler, Locarno, Fascism and the threat of war aroused hardly a flicker of interest locally, but the decision of the Football Association to stop publishing their fixtures in advance (this was an attempt to quell the Football Pools) flung all Yorkshire into a storm of fury. And then there is the queer spectacle of modern electrical science showering miracles upon people with empty bellies. You may shiver all night for lack of bedclothes, but in the morning you can go to the public library and read the news that has been telegraphed for your benefit from San Francisco and Singapore. Twenty million people are underfed but literally everyone in

England has access to a radio. What we have lost in food we have gained in electricity. Whole sections of the working class who have been plundered of all they really need are being compensated, in part, by cheap luxuries which mitigate the surface of life.

Do you consider all this desirable ? No, I don't. But it may be that the psychological adjustment which the working class are visibly making is the best they could make in the circumstances. They have neither turned revolutionary nor lost their self-respect; merely they have kept their tempers and settled down to make the best of things on a fish-and-chip standard. The alternative would be God knows what continued agonies of despair; or it might be attempted insurrections which, in a strongly governed country like England, could only lead to futile massacres and a régime of savage repression.

Of course the post-war development of cheap luxuries has been a very fortunate thing for our rulers. It is quite likely that fish and chips, art-silk stockings, tinned salmon, cut-price chocolate (five two-ounce bars for sixpence), the movies, the radio, strong tea and the Football Pools have between them averted revolution. Therefore we are sometimes told that the whole thing is an astute manœuvre by the governing class—a sort of " bread and circuses " business—to hold the unemployed down. What I have seen of our governing class does not convince me that they have that much intelligence. The thing has happened, but by an unconscious process—the quite natural interaction between the manufacturer's need for a market and the need of half-starved people for cheap palliatives.

CHAPTER VI

WHEN I WAS A SMALL BOY AT SCHOOL a lecturer used to come once a term and deliver excellent lectures on famous battles of the past, such as Blenheim, Austerlitz, etc. He was fond of quoting Napoleon's maxim " An army marches on its stomach," and at the end of his lecture he would suddenly turn to us and demand, " What's the most important thing in the world ? " We were expected to shout " Food ! " and if we did not do so he was disappointed.

Obviously he was right in a way. A human being is primarily a bag for putting food into; the other functions and faculties may be more godlike, but in point of time they come afterwards. A man dies and is buried, and all his words and actions are forgotten, but the food he has eaten lives after him in the sound or rotten bones of his children. I think it could be plausibly argued that changes of diet are more important than changes of dynasty or even of religion. The Great War, for instance, could never have happened if tinned food had not been invented. And the history of the past four hundred years in England would have been immensely different if it had not been for the introduction of root-crops and various other vegetables at the end of the Middle Ages, and a little later the introduction of non-alcoholic drinks (tea, coffee, cocoa) and also of distilled liquors to which the beer-drinking English were not accustomed. Yet it is curious how seldom the all-importance of food is recognised. You see statues everywhere to politicians, poets, bishops, but none to cooks or bacon-curers or market-gardeners. The Emperor Charles V is said to have erected a statue to the inventor of bloaters, but that is the only case I can think of at the moment.

So perhaps the really important thing about the unemployed, the really basic thing if you look to the future, is the diet they are living on. As I said earlier, the average unemployed family lives on an income of round about thirty shillings a week, of which at least a quarter goes in rent. It is worth considering in some detail how the remaining money is spent. I have here a budget which was made out for me by an unemployed miner and his wife. I asked them to make a list which represented as exactly as possible their expenditure in a typical week. This man's allowance was thirty-two shillings a week, and besides his wife he had two children, one aged two years and five months and the other ten months. Here is the list:

	s.	d.
Rent	9	0½
Clothing Club	3	0
Coal	2	0
Gas	1	3
Milk	0	10½
Union fees	0	3
Insurance (on the children) . .	0	2
Meat	2	6
Flour (2 stone)	3	4
Yeast	0	4
Potatoes	1	0
Dripping	0	10
Margarine	0	10
Bacon	1	2
Sugar	1	9

	s.	d.
Tea	1	0
Jam	0	7½
Peas and cabbage . . .	0	6
Carrots and onions . . .	0	4
Quaker oats.	0	4½
Soap, powders, blue, etc. . .	0	10
Total . . £1	12	0

In addition to this, three packets of dried milk were supplied weekly for the baby by the Infants' Welfare Clinic.

One or two comments are needed here. To begin with, the list leaves out a great deal—blacking, pepper, salt, vinegar, matches, kindling-wood, razor blades, replacements of utensils and wear and tear of furniture and bedding, to name the first few that come to mind. Any money spent on these would mean reduction on some other item. A more serious charge is tobacco. This man happened to be a small smoker, but even so his tobacco would hardly cost less than a shilling a week, meaning a further reduction on food. The " clothing clubs " into which unemployed people pay so much a week are run by big drapers in all the industrial towns. Without them it would be impossible for unemployed people to buy new clothes at all. I don't know whether or not they buy bedding through these clubs. This particular family, as I happen to know, possessed next to no bedding.

In the above list, if you allow a shilling for tobacco and deduct this and the other non-food items, you are left with sixteen and fivepence halfpenny. Call it sixteen shillings and leave the baby out of account—for the baby was getting its weekly packets of milk from the Welfare Clinic. This sixteen shillings has got to provide the entire nourishment, *including fuel*, of three persons, two of them adult. The first question is whether it is even theoretically possible for three persons to be properly nourished on sixteen shillings a week. When the dispute over the Means Test was in progress there was a disgusting public wrangle about the minimum weekly sum on which a human being could keep alive. So far as I remember, one school of dietitians worked it out at five and ninepence, while another school, more generous, put it at five and ninepence halfpenny. After this there were letters to the papers from a number of people who claimed to be feeding themselves on four shillings a week. Here is a weekly budget (it was printed in the *New Statesman* and also in the *News of the World*) which I picked out from among a number of others:

	s.	d.
3 wholemeal loaves	1	0
½ lb. margarine	0	2½
½ lb. dripping	0	3
1 lb. cheese	0	7
1 lb. onions	0	1½
1 lb. carrots	0	1½
1 lb. broken biscuits	0	4
2 lb. dates	0	6
1 tin evaporated milk . . .	0	5
10 oranges	0	5
Total . . .	3	11½

Please notice that this budget contains *nothing for fuel*. In fact, the writer explicitly stated that he could not afford to buy fuel and ate all his food raw. Whether the letter was genuine or a hoax does not matter at the moment. What I think will be admitted is that this list represents about as wise an expenditure as could be contrived; if you *had* to live on three and elevenpence halfpenny a week, you could hardly extract more food-value from it than that. So perhaps it is possible to feed yourself adequately on the P.A.C. allowance if you concentrate on essential foodstuffs ; but not otherwise.

Now compare this list with the unemployed miner's budget that I gave earlier. The miner's family spend only tenpence a week on green vegetables and tenpence halfpenny on milk (remember that one of them is a child less than three years old), and nothing on fruit; but they spend one and nine on sugar (about eight pounds of sugar, that is) and a shilling on tea. The half-crown spent on meat *might* represent a small joint and the materials for a stew; probably as often as not it would represent four or five tins of bully beef. The basis of their diet, therefore, is white bread and margarine, corned beef, sugared tea and potatoes—an appalling diet. Would it not be better if they spent more money on wholesome things like oranges and wholemeal bread or if they even, like the writer of the letter to the *New Statesman*, saved on fuel and ate their carrots raw ? Yes, it would, but the point is that no ordinary human being is ever going to do such a thing. The ordinary human being would sooner starve than live on brown bread and raw carrots. And the peculiar evil is this, that the less money you have, the less inclined you feel to spend it on wholesome food. A millionaire may enjoy breakfasting off orange juice and Ryvita biscuits; an unemployed man doesn't. Here the tendency of which I spoke at the end of the last chapter comes into play. When you are unemployed, which is to say when you are underfed, harassed, bored and miserable, you don't *want* to eat dull wholesome food. You want something a little bit " tasty." There is always some cheaply

pleasant thing to tempt you. Let's have three pennorth
of chips ! Run out and buy us a twopenny ice-cream !
Put the kettle on and we'll all have a nice cup of tea !
That is how your mind works when you are at the P.A.C.
level. White bread-and-marg and sugared tea don't
nourish you to any extent, but they are *nicer* (at least
most people think so) than brown bread-and-dripping
and cold water. Unemployment is an endless misery
that has got to be constantly palliated, and especially
with tea, the Englishman's opium. A cup of tea or even
an aspirin is much better as a temporary stimulant
than a crust of brown bread.

The results of all this are visible in a physical
degeneracy which you can study directly, by using your
eyes, or inferentially, by having a look at the vital
statistics. The physical average in the industrial towns
is terribly low, lower even than in London. In Sheffield
you have the feeling of walking among a population of
troglodytes. The miners are splendid men, but they are
usually small, and the mere fact that their muscles are
toughened by constant work does not mean that their
children start life with a better physique. In any case
the miners are physically the pick of the population. The
most obvious sign of under-nourishment is the badness
of everybody's teeth. In Lancashire you would have to
look for a long time before you saw a working-class
person with good natural teeth. Indeed, you see very
few people with natural teeth at all, apart from the
children; and even the children's teeth have a frail
bluish appearance which means, I suppose, calcium
deficiency. Several dentists have told me that in industrial districts a person over thirty with any of his or her
own teeth is coming to be an abnormality. In Wigan
various people gave me their opinion that it is best to

" get shut of " your teeth as early in life as possible.
" Teeth is just a misery," one woman said to me. In one
house where I stayed there were, apart from myself, five
people, the oldest being forty-three and the youngest
a boy of fifteen. Of these the boy was the only one who
possessed a single tooth of his own, and his teeth were
obviously not going to last long. As for the vital statistics,
the fact that in any large industrial town the death rate
and infant mortality rate of the poorest quarters are
always about double those of the well-to-do residential
quarters—a good deal more than double in some cases—
hardly needs commenting on.

Of course one ought not to imagine that the prevailing
bad physique is due solely to unemployment, for it is
probable that the physical average has been declining
all over England for a long time past, and not merely
among the unemployed in the industrial areas. This cannot be proved statistically, but it is a conclusion that is
forced upon you if you use your eyes, even in rural places
and even in a prosperous town like London. On the day
when King George V's body passed through London on
its way to Westminster, I happened to be caught for an
hour or two in the crowd in Trafalgar Square. It was
impossible, looking about one then, not to be struck by
the physical degeneracy of modern England. The people
surrounding me were *not* working-class people for the
most part; they were the shopkeeper-commercial-
traveller type, with a sprinkling of the well-to-do. But
what a set they looked ! Puny limbs, sickly faces, under
the weeping London sky ! Hardly a well-built man or
a decent-looking woman, and not a fresh complexion
anywhere. As the King's coffin went by, the men took
off their hats, and a friend who was in the crowd at the
other side of the Strand said to me afterwards, " The

only touch of colour anywhere was the bald heads.''
Even the Guards, it seemed to me—there was a squad
of guardsmen marching beside the coffin—were not
what they used to be. Where are the monstrous men
with chests like barrels and moustaches like the wings
of eagles who strode across my childhood's gaze twenty
or thirty years ago? Buried, I suppose, in the Flanders
mud. In their place there are these pale-faced boys who
have been picked for their height and consequently look
like hop-poles in overcoats—the truth being that in
modern England a man over six feet high is usually skin
and bone and not much else. If the English physique
has declined, this is no doubt partly due to the fact that
the Great War carefully selected the million best men
in England and slaughtered them, largely before they
had had time to breed. But the process must have begun
earlier than that, and it must be due ultimately to
unhealthy ways of living, i.e. to industrialism. I don't
mean the habit of living in towns—probably the town
is healthier than the country, in many ways—but the
modern industrial technique which provides you with
cheap substitutes for everything. We may find in the
long run that tinned food is a deadlier weapon than the
machine gun.

It is unfortunate that the English working class—the
English nation generally, for that matter—are exceptionally ignorant about and wasteful of food. I have pointed
out elsewhere how civilised is a French navvy's idea of
a meal compared with an Englishman's, and I cannot
believe that you would ever see such wastage in a French
house as you habitually see in English ones. Of course,
in the very poorest homes, where everybody is unemployed, you don't see much actual waste, but those
who can afford to waste food often do so. I could give

startling instances of this. Even the Northern habit of baking one's own bread is slightly wasteful in itself, because an overworked woman cannot bake more than once or, at most, twice a week and it is impossible to tell beforehand how much bread will be wasted, so that a certain amount generally has to be thrown away. The usual thing is to bake six large loaves and twelve small ones at a time. All this is part of the old, generous English attitude to life, and it is an amiable quality, but a disastrous one at the present moment.

English working people everywhere, so far as I know, refuse brown bread; it is usually impossible to buy wholemeal bread in a working-class district. They sometimes give the reason that brown bread is " dirty." I suspect the real reason is that in the past brown bread has been confused with black bread, which is traditionally associated with Popery and wooden shoes. (They have plenty of Popery and wooden shoes in Lancashire. A pity they haven't the black bread as well !) But the English palate, especially the working-class palate, now rejects good food almost automatically. The number of people who *prefer* tinned peas and tinned fish to real peas and real fish must be increasing every year, and plenty of people who could afford real milk in their tea would much sooner have tinned milk—even that dreadful tinned milk which is made of sugar and cornflour and has UNFIT FOR BABIES on the tin in huge letters. In some districts efforts are now being made to teach the unemployed more about food-values and more about the intelligent spending of money. When you hear of a thing like this you feel yourself torn both ways. I have heard a Communist speaker on the platform grow very angry about it. In London, he said, parties of Society dames now have the cheek to walk into East End houses and give shopping-lessons to the wives of the unemployed. He gave this as an instance of the mentality of the English governing class. First you condemn a family to live on thirty shillings a week, and then you have the damned impertinence to tell them how they are to spend their money. He was quite right—I agree heartily. Yet all the same it *is* a pity that, merely for the lack of a proper tradition, people should pour muck like tinned milk down their throats and not even know that it is inferior to the product of the cow.

I doubt, however, whether the unemployed would ultimately benefit if they learned to spend their money more economically. For it is only the fact that they are *not* economical that keeps their allowances so high. An Englishman on the P.A.C. gets fifteen shillings a week because fifteen shillings is the smallest sum on which he can conceivably keep alive. If he were, say, an Indian or Japanese coolie, who can live on rice and onions, he wouldn't get fifteen shillings a week—he would be lucky if he got fifteen shillings a month. Our unemployment allowances, miserable though they are, are framed to suit a population with very high standards and not much notion of economy. If the unemployed learned to be better managers they would be visibly better off, and I fancy it would not be long before the dole was docked correspondingly.

There is one great mitigation of unemployment in the North, and that is the cheapness of fuel. Anywhere in the coal areas the retail price of coal is about one and sixpence a hundredweight; in the South of England it is about half a crown. Moreover, miners in work can usually buy coal direct from the pit at eight or nine shillings a ton, and those who have a cellar in their homes sometimes store a ton at a time and sell it (illicitly, I suppose) to those who are out of work. But apart from this there is immense and systematic thieving of coal by the unemployed. I call it thieving because technically it is that, though it does no harm to anybody. In the " dirt " that is sent up from the pits there is a certain amount of broken coal, and unemployed people spend a lot of time in picking it out of the slag-heaps. All day long over those strange grey mountains you see people wandering to and fro with sacks and baskets among the sulphurous smoke (many slag-heaps are on fire under the surface), prising out the tiny nuggets of coal which are buried here and there. You meet men coming away, wheeling strange and wonderful home-made bicycles—bicycles made of rusty parts picked off refuse-tips, without saddles, without chains and almost always without tyres—across which are slung bags containing perhaps half a hundredweight of coal, fruit of half a day's searching. In times of strikes, when every-body is short of fuel, the miners turn out with pick and shovel and burrow into the slag-heaps, whence the hummocky appearance which most slag-heaps have. During long strikes, in places where there are outcrops of coal, they have sunk surface mines and carried them scores of yards into the earth.

In Wigan the competition among unemployed people for the waste coal has become so fierce that it has led to an extraordinary custom called " scrambling for the coal," which is well worth seeing. Indeed I rather wonder that it has never been filmed. An unemployed miner took me to see it one afternoon. We got to the place, a mountain range of ancient slag-heaps with a railway running through the valley below. A couple of hundred ragged men, each with a sack and coal-hammer strapped under his coat-tails, were waiting on the " broo." When the dirt comes up from the pit it is loaded on to trucks and an engine runs these to the top of another slag-heap a quarter of a mile away and there leaves them. The process of " scrambling for the coal " consists in getting on to the train while it is moving; any truck which you have succeeded in boarding while it is in motion counts as " your " truck. Presently the train hove in sight. With a wild yell a hundred men dashed down the slope to catch her as she rounded the bend. Even at the bend the train was making twenty miles an hour. The men hurled themselves upon it, caught hold of the rings at the rear of the trucks and hoisted themselves up by way of the bumpers, five or ten of them on each truck. The driver took no notice. He drove up to the top of the slag-heap, uncoupled the trucks and ran the engine back to the pit, presently returning with a fresh string of trucks. There was the same wild rush of ragged figures as before. In the end only about fifty men had failed to get on to either train.

We walked up to the top of the slag-heap. The men were shovelling the dirt out of the trucks, while down below their wives and children were kneeling, swiftly scrabbling with their hands in the damp dirt and picking out lumps of coal the size of an egg or smaller. You would see a woman pounce on a tiny fragment of stuff, wipe it on her apron, scrutinise it to make sure it was coal and pop it jealously into her sack. Of course, when you are boarding a truck you don't know beforehand what is in it; it may be actual " dirt " from the roads or it may merely be shale from the roofing. If it is a shale truck there will be no coal in it, but there occurs among the shale another inflammable rock called cannel, which looks very like ordinary shale but is slightly darker and is known by splitting in parallel lines, like slate. It makes tolerable fuel, not good enough to be commercially valuable but good enough to be eagerly sought after by the unemployed. The miners on the shale trucks were picking out the cannel and splitting it up with their hammers. Down at the bottom of the " broo " the people who had failed to get on to either train were gleaning the tiny chips of coal that came rolling down from above —fragments no bigger than a hazel nut, these, but the people were glad enough to get them.

We stayed there till the train was empty. In a couple of hours the people had picked the dirt over to the last grain. They slung their sacks over shoulder or bicycle, and started on the two-mile trudge back to Wigan. Most of the families had gathered about half a hundredweight of coal or cannel, so that between them they must have stolen five or ten tons of fuel. This business of robbing the dirt trains takes place every day in Wigan, at any rate in winter, and at more collieries than one. It is of course extremely dangerous. No one was hurt the afternoon I was there, but a man had had both his legs cut off a few weeks earlier, and another man lost several fingers a week later. Technically it is stealing but, as everybody knows, if the coal were not stolen it would simply be wasted. Now and again, for form's sake, the colliery companies prosecute somebody for coal-picking, and in that morning's issue of the local paper there was a paragraph saying that two men had been fined ten shillings. But no notice is taken of the prosecutions—in fact, one of the men named in the paper was there that afternoon—and the coal-pickers subscribe among themselves to pay the fines. The thing is taken for granted. Everyone knows that the unemployed have got to get fuel somehow. So every afternoon several hundred men risk their necks and several hundred women scrabble in the mud for hours—and all for half a hundredweight of inferior fuel, value ninepence.

That scene stays in my mind as one of my pictures of Lancashire: the dumpy, shawled women, with their sacking aprons and their heavy black clogs, kneeling in the cindery mud and the bitter wind, searching eagerly for tiny chips of coal. They are glad enough to do it. In winter they are desperate for fuel; it is more important almost than food. Meanwhile all round, as far as the eye can see, are the slag-heaps and hoisting gear of collieries, and not one of those collieries can sell all the coal it is capable of producing. This ought to appeal to Major Douglas.

CHAPTER VII

As you travel northward your eye, accustomed to the South or East, does not notice much difference until you are beyond Birmingham. In Coventry you might as well be in Finsbury Park, and the Bull Ring in Birmingham is not unlike Norwich Market, and between all the towns of the Midlands there stretches a villa-civilisation indistinguishable from that of the South. It is only when you get a little further north, to the pottery towns and beyond, that you begin to encounter the real ugliness of industrialism—an ugliness so frightful and so arresting that you are obliged, as it were, to come to terms with it.

A slag-heap is at best a hideous thing, because it is so planless and functionless. It is something just dumped on the earth, like the emptying of a giant's dust-bin. On the outskirts of the mining towns there are frightful landscapes where your horizon is ringed completely round by jagged grey mountains, and underfoot is mud and ashes and overhead the steel cables where tubs of dirt travel slowly across miles of country. Often the slag-heaps are on fire, and at night you can see the red rivulets of fire winding this way and that, and also the slow-moving blue flames of sulphur, which always seem on the point of expiring and always spring out again. Even when a slag-heap sinks, as it does ultimately, only an evil brown grass grows on it, and it retains its hummocky surface. One in the slums of Wigan, used as a playground, looks like a choppy sea suddenly frozen; " the flock mattress," it is called locally. Even centuries hence when the plough drives over the places where coal was once mined, the sites of ancient slag-heaps will still be distinguishable from an aeroplane.

I remember a winter afternoon in the dreadful environs of Wigan. All round was the lunar landscape of slag-heaps, and to the north, through the passes, as it were, between the mountains of slag, you could see the factory chimneys sending out their plumes of smoke. The canal path was a mixture of cinders and frozen mud, criss-crossed by the imprints of innumerable clogs, and all round, as far as the slag-heaps in the distance, stretched the " flashes "—pools of stagnant water that has seeped into the hollows caused by the subsidence of ancient pits. It was horribly cold. The " flashes " were covered with ice the colour of raw umber, the bargemen were muffled to the eyes in sacks, the lock gates wore beards of ice. It seemed a world from which vegetation had been banished; nothing existed except smoke, shale, ice, mud, ashes and foul water. But even Wigan is beautiful compared with Sheffield. Sheffield, I suppose, could justly claim to be called the ugliest town in the Old World: its inhabitants, who want it to be pre-eminent in everything, very likely do make that claim for it. It has a population of half a million and it contains fewer decent buildings than the average East Anglian village of five hundred. And the stench ! If at rare moments you stop smelling sulphur it is because you have begun smelling gas. Even the shallow river that runs through the town is usually bright yellow with some chemical or other. Once I halted in the street and counted the factory chimneys I could see; there were thirty-three of them, but there would have been far more if the air had not been obscured by smoke. One scene especially lingers in my mind. A frightful patch of waste ground (somehow, up there, a patch of waste ground attains a squalor that would be impossible even in London) trampled bare of grass and littered with newspapers and old saucepans. To the right an isolated row of gaunt four-roomed houses, dark red, blackened by smoke. To the left an interminable vista of factory chimneys, chimney beyond chimney, fading away into a dim blackish haze. Behind me a railway embankment made of the slag from furnaces. In front, across the patch of waste ground, a cubical building of red and yellow brick, with the sign " Thomas Grocock, Haulage Contractor."

At night, when you cannot see the hideous shapes of the houses and the blackness of everything, a town like Sheffield assumes a kind of sinister magnificence. Sometimes the drifts of smoke are rosy with sulphur, and serrated flames, like circular saws, squeeze themselves out from beneath the cowls of the foundry chimneys. Through the open doors of foundries you see fiery serpents of iron being hauled to and fro by redlit boys, and you hear the whizz and thump of steam hammers and the scream of the iron under the blow. The pottery towns are almost equally ugly in a pettier way. Right in among the rows of tiny blackened houses, part of the street as it were, are the " pot banks "—conical brick chimneys like gigantic burgundy bottles buried in the soil and belching their smoke almost in your face. You come upon monstrous clay chasms hundreds of feet across and almost as deep, with little rusty tubs creeping on chain railways up one side, and on the other workmen clinging like samphire-gatherers and cutting into the face of the cliff with their picks. I passed that way in snowy weather, and even the snow was black. The best thing one can say for the pottery towns is that they are fairly small and stop abruptly. Less than ten miles away you can stand in undefiled country, on the almost naked hills, and the pottery towns are only a smudge in the distance.

When you contemplate such ugliness as this, there are two questions that strike you. First, is it inevitable? Secondly, does it matter?

I do not believe that there is anything inherently and unavoidably ugly about industrialism. A factory or even a gasworks is not obliged of its own nature to be ugly, any more than a palace or a dog-kennel or a cathedral. It all depends on the architectural tradition of the period. The industrial towns of the North are ugly because they happen to have been built at a time when modern methods of steel-construction and smoke-abatement were unknown, and when everyone was too busy making money to think about anything else. They go on being ugly largely because the Northerners have got used to that kind of thing and do not notice it. Many of the people in Sheffield or Manchester, if they smelled the air along the Cornish cliffs, would probably declare that it had no taste in it. But since the war, industry has tended to shift southward and in doing so has grown almost comely. The typical post-war factory is not a gaunt barrack or an awful chaos of blackness and belching chimneys; it is a glittering white structure of concrete, glass and steel, surrounded by green lawns and beds of tulips. Look at the factories you pass as you travel out of London on the G.W.R.; they may not be æsthetic triumphs but certainly they are not ugly in the same way as the Sheffield gasworks. But in any case, though the ugliness of industrialism is

the most obvious thing about it and the thing every
newcomer exclaims against, I doubt whether it is
centrally important. And perhaps it is not even desirable, industrialism being what it is, that it should learn
to disguise itself as something else. As Mr. Aldous
Huxley has truly remarked, a dark Satanic mill ought
to look like a dark Satanic mill and not like the temple
of mysterious and splendid gods. Moreover, even in the
worst of the industrial towns one sees a great deal that is
not ugly in the narrow æsthetic sense. A belching
chimney or a stinking slum is repulsive chiefly because
it implies warped lives and ailing children. Look at it
from a purely æsthetic standpoint and it may have a
certain macabre appeal. I find that anything out-
rageously strange generally ends by fascinating me
even when I abominate it. The landscapes of Burma,
which, when I was among them, so appalled me as to
assume the qualities of nightmare, afterwards stayed so
hauntingly in my mind that I was obliged to write a
novel about them to get rid of them. (In all novels
about the East the scenery is the real subject-matter.)
It would probably be quite easy to extract a sort of
beauty, as Arnold Bennett did, from the blackness of
the industrial towns; one can easily imagine Baudelaire,
for instance, writing a poem about a slag-heap. But the
beauty or ugliness of industrialism hardly matters. Its
real evil lies far deeper and is quite ineradicable. It is
important to remember this, because there is always a
temptation to think that industrialism is harmless so
long as it is clean and orderly.

But when you go to the industrial North you are
conscious, quite apart from the unfamiliar scenery, of
entering a strange country. This is partly because of
certain real differences which do exist, but still more

because of the North-South antithesis which has been
rubbed into us for such a long time past. There exists
in England a curious cult of Northernness, a sort of
Northern snobbishness. A Yorkshireman in the South
will always take care to let you know that he regards
you as an inferior. If you ask him why, he will explain
that it is only in the North that life is " real " life, that
the industrial work done in the North is the only " real "
work, that the North is inhabited by " real " people,
the South merely by rentiers and their parasites. The
Northerner has " grit," he is grim, " dour," plucky,
warm-hearted and democratic; the Southerner is snobbish, effeminate and lazy—that at any rate is the theory.
Hence the Southerner goes north, at any rate for the
first time, with the vague inferiority-complex of a civilised
man venturing among savages, while the Yorkshireman,
like the Scotchman, comes to London in the spirit of a
barbarian out for loot. And feelings of this kind, which
are the result of tradition, are not affected by visible
facts. Just as an Englishman five feet four inches high
and twenty nine inches round the chest feels that as an
Englishman he is the physical superior of Carnera
(Carnera being a Dago), so also with the Northerner
and the Southerner. I remember a weedy little Yorkshireman who would almost certainly have run away if a
fox-terrier had snapped at him, telling me that in the
South of England he felt " like a wild invader." But
the cult is often adopted by people who are not by
birth Northerners themselves. A year or two ago
a friend of mine, brought up in the South but now
living in the North, was driving me through Suffolk
in a car. We passed through a rather beautiful
village. He glanced disapprovingly at the cottages
and said:

" Of course most of the villages in Yorkshire are hideous ; but the Yorkshiremen are splendid chaps. Down here it's just the other way about—beautiful villages and rotten people. All the people in those cottages there are worthless, absolutely worthless."

I could not help enquiring whether he happened to know anybody in that village. No, he did not know them ; but because this was East Anglia they were obviously worthless. Another friend of mine, again a Southerner by birth, loses no opportunity of praising the North to the detriment of the South. Here is an extract from one of his letters to me :

" I am in Clitheroe, Lancs. . . . I think running water is much more attractive in moor and mountain country than in the fat and sluggish South. ' The smug and silver Trent,' Shakespeare says ; and the South-er the smugger, I say."

Here you have an interesting example of the Northern cult. Not only are you and I and everyone else in the South of England written off as " fat and sluggish," but even water, when it gets north of a certain latitude, ceases to be H_2O and becomes something mystically superior. But the interest of this passage is that its writer is an extremely intelligent man of " advanced " opinions who would have nothing but contempt for nationalism in its ordinary form. Put to him some such proposition as " One Britisher is worth three foreigners," and he would repudiate it with horror. But when it is a question of North versus South, he is quite ready to generalise. *All* nationalistic distinctions—all claims to be better than somebody else because you have a different-shaped skull or speak a different dialect—are entirely spurious, but they are important so long as people believe in them. There is no doubt about the Englishman's inbred conviction that those who live to the south of him are his inferiors; even our foreign policy is governed by it to some extent. I think therefore, that it is worth pointing out when and why it came into being.

When nationalism first became a religion, the English looked at the map, and, noticing that their island lay very high in the Northern Hemisphere, evolved the pleasing theory that the further north you live the more virtuous you become. The histories I was given when I was a little boy generally started off by explaining in the naïvest way that a cold climate made people energetic while a hot one made them lazy, and hence the defeat of the Spanish Armada. This nonsense about the superior energy of the English (actually the laziest people in Europe) has been current for at least a hundred years. " Better is it for us," writes a Quarterly Reviewer of 1827, " to be condemned to labour for our country's good than to luxuriate amid olives, vines and vices." " Olives, vines and vices " sums up the normal English attitude towards the Latin races. In the mythology of Carlyle, Creasey, etc., the Northerner (" Teutonic," later " Nordic ") is pictured as a hefty, vigorous chap with blond moustaches and pure morals, while the Southerner is sly, cowardly and licentious. This theory was never pushed to its logical end, which would have meant assuming that the finest people in the world were the Eskimos, but it did involve admitting that the people who lived to the north of us were superior to ourselves. Hence, partly, the cult of Scotland and of Scotch things which has so deeply marked English life during the past fifty years. But it was the industrialisation of the North that gave the North-South antithesis its peculiar slant. Until comparatively recently the northern part of England was the backward and feudal part, and such industry as existed was concentrated in London and the South-East. In the Civil War, for instance, roughly speaking a war of money versus feudalism, the North and West were for the King and the South and East for the Parliament. But with the increasing use of coal industry passed to the North, and there grew up a new type of man, the self-made Northern business man—the Mr. Rouncewell and Mr. Bounderby of Dickens. The Northern business man, with his hateful " get on or get out " philosophy, was the dominant figure of the nine-teenth century, and as a sort of tyrannical corpse he rules us still. This is the type deified by Arnold Bennett— the type who starts off with half a crown and ends up with fifty thousand pounds, and whose chief pride is to be an even greater boor after he has made his money than before. On analysis his sole virtue turns out to be a talent for making money. We were bidden to admire him because though he might be narrow-minded, sordid, ignorant, grasping and uncouth, he had " grit," he " got on "; in other words, he knew how to make money.

This kind of cant is nowadays a pure anachronism, for the Northern business man is no longer prosperous. But traditions are not killed by facts, and the tradition of Northern " grit " lingers. It is still dimly felt that a Northerner will " get on," i.e. make money, where a Southerner will fail. At the back of the mind of every Yorkshireman and every Scotchman who comes to London is a sort of Dick Whittington picture of himself as the boy who starts off by selling newspapers and ends up as Lord Mayor, And that, really, is at the bottom of his bumptiousness. But where one can make a great mistake is in imagining that this feeling extends to the genuine working class. When I first went to Yorkshire, some years ago, I imagined that I was going to a country of boors. I was used to the London Yorkshireman with his interminable harangues and his pride in the supposed raciness of his dialect (" ' A stitch in time saves nine,' as we say in the West Riding "), and I expected to meet with a good deal of rudeness. But I met with nothing of the kind, and least of all among the miners. Indeed the Lancashire and Yorkshire miners treated me with a kindness and courtesy that were even embarrassing; for if there is one type of man to whom I do feel myself inferior, it is a coal-miner. Certainly no one showed any sign of despising me for coming from a different part of the country. This has its importance when one remembers that the English regional snobberies are nationalism in miniature; for it suggests that place-snobbery is not a working-class characteristic.

There is nevertheless a real difference between North and South, and there is at least a tinge of truth in that picture of Southern England as one enormous Brighton inhabited by lounge-lizards. For climatic reasons the parasitic dividend-drawing class tend to settle in the South. In a Lancashire cotton-town you could probably go for months on end without once hearing an " educated " accent, whereas there can hardly be a town in the South of England where you could throw a brick without hitting the niece of a bishop. Consequently, with no petty gentry to set the pace, the bourgeoisification of the working class, though it is taking place in the North, is taking place more slowly. All the Northern accents, for instance, persist strongly, while the Southern ones are collapsing before the movies and the B.B.C. Hence your " educated " accent stamps you rather as a foreigner than as a chunk of the petty gentry; and this is an immense advantage, for it makes it much easier to get into contact with the working class.

But is it ever possible to be really intimate with the working class ? I shall have to discuss that later; I will only say here that I do not think it is possible. But undoubtedly it is easier in the North than it would be in the South to meet working-class people on approximately equal terms. It is fairly easy to live in a miner's house and be accepted as one of the family; with, say, a farm labourer in the Southern counties it probably would be impossible. I have seen just enough of the working class to avoid idealising them, but I do know that you can learn a great deal in a working-class home, if only you can get there. The essential point is that your middle-class ideals and prejudices are tested by contact with others which are not necessarily better but are certainly different.

Take for instance the different attitude towards the family. A working-class family hangs together as a middle-class one does, but the relationship is far less tyrannical. A working-man has not that deadly weight of family prestige hanging round his neck like a millstone. I have pointed out earlier that a middle-class person goes utterly to pieces under the influence of poverty; and this is generally due to the behaviour of his family—to the fact that he has scores of relations nagging and badgering him night and day for failing to " get on." The fact that the working class know how to combine and the middle class don't is probably due to their different conceptions of family loyalty. You cannot have an effective trade-union of middle-class workers, because in times of strikes almost every middle-class wife would be egging her husband on to blackleg and get the other fellow's job. Another working-class characteristic, disconcerting at first, is their plain-spokenness towards anyone they regard as an equal. If you offer a working-man something he doesn't want, he tells you that he doesn't want it; a middle-class person would accept it to avoid giving offence. And again, take the working-class attitude towards " education." How different it is from ours, and how immensely sounder! Working-people often have a vague reverence for learning in others, but where " education " touches their own lives they see through it and reject it by a healthy instinct. The time was when I used to lament over quite imaginary pictures of lads of fourteen dragged protesting from their lessons and set to work at dismal jobs. It seemed to me dreadful that the doom of a " job " should descend upon anyone at fourteen. Of course I know now that there is not one working-class boy in a thousand who does not pine for the day when he will leave school. He wants to be doing real work, not wasting his time on ridiculous rubbish like history and geography. To the working class, the notion of staying at school till you are nearly grown-up seems merely contemptible and unmanly. The idea of a great big boy of eighteen, who ought to be bringing a pound a week home to his parents, going to school in a ridiculous uniform and even being caned for not doing his lessons! Just fancy a working-class boy of eighteen allowing himself to be caned! He is a man when the other is still a baby. Ernest Pontifex, in Samuel Butler's *Way of All Flesh*, after he had had a few glimpses of real life, looked back on his public school and university education and found it a " sickly, debilitating debauch." There is much in middle-class life that looks sickly and debilitating when you see it from a working-class angle.

In a working-class home—I am not thinking at the moment of the unemployed, but of comparatively prosperous homes—you breathe a warm, decent, deeply human atmosphere which it is not so easy to find elsewhere. I should say that a manual worker, if he is in steady work and drawing good wages—an " if " which gets bigger and bigger—has a better chance of being happy than an " educated " man. His home life seems to fall more naturally into a sane and comely shape. I have often been struck by the peculiar easy completeness, the perfect symmetry as it were, of a working-class interior at its best. Especially on winter evenings after tea, when the fire glows in the open range and dances mirrored in the steel fender, when Father, in shirt-sleeves, sits in the rocking chair at one side of the fire reading the racing finals, and Mother sits on the other with her sewing, and the children are happy with a pennorth of mint humbugs, and the dog lolls roasting himself on the rag mat—it is a good place to be in, provided that you can be not only in it but sufficiently *of* it to be taken for granted.

This scene is still reduplicated in a majority of English homes, though not in so many as before the war. Its happiness depends mainly upon one question—whether Father is in work. But notice that the picture I have called up, of a working-class family sitting round the coal fire after kippers and strong tea, belongs only to our own moment of time and could not belong either to the future or the past. Skip forward two hundred years into the Utopian future, and the scene is totally different. Hardly one of the things I have imagined will still be there. In that age when there is no manual labour and everyone is " educated," it is hardly likely that Father will still be a rough man with enlarged hands who likes to sit in shirt-sleeves and says " Ah wur coomin' oop street." And there won't be a coal fire in the grate, only some kind of invisible heater. The furniture will be made of rubber, glass and steel. If there are still such things as evening papers there will certainly be no racing news in them, for gambling will be meaningless in a world where there is no poverty and the horse will have vanished from the face of the earth. Dogs, too, will have been suppressed on grounds of hygiene. And there won't be so many children, either, if the birth-controllers have their way. But move backwards into the Middle Ages and you are in a world almost equally foreign. A windowless hut, a wood fire which smokes in your face because there is no chimney, mouldy bread, " Poor John," lice, scurvy, a yearly childbirth and a yearly child-death, and the priest terrifying you with tales of Hell.

Curiously enough it is *not* the triumphs of modern engineering, nor the radio, nor the cinematograph, nor the five thousand novels which are published yearly, nor the crowds at Ascot and the Eton and Harrow match, but the memory of working-class interiors—especially as I sometimes saw them in my childhood before the war, when England was still prosperous—that reminds me that our age has not been altogether a bad one to live in.

PART II

CHAPTER VIII

THE ROAD from Mandalay to Wigan is a long one and the reasons for taking it are not immediately clear.

In the earlier chapters of this book I have given a rather fragmentary account of various things I saw in the coal areas of Lancashire and Yorkshire. I went there partly because I wanted to see what mass-unemployment is like at its worst, partly in order to see the most typical section of the English working class at close quarters. This was necessary to me as part of my approach to Socialism. For before you can be sure whether you are genuinely in favour of Socialism, you have got to decide whether things at present are tolerable or not tolerable, and you have got to take up a definite attitude on the terribly difficult issue of class. Here I shall have to digress and explain how my own attitude towards the class question was developed. Obviously this involves writing a certain amount of autobiography, and I would not do it if I did not think that I am sufficiently typical of my class, or rather sub-caste, to have a certain symptomatic importance.

I was born into what you might describe as the lower-upper-middle class. The upper-middle class, which had its heyday in the 'eighties and 'nineties, with Kipling as its poet laureate, was a sort of mound of wreckage left behind when the tide of Victorian prosperity receded. Or perhaps it would be better to change the metaphor and describe it not as a mound but as a layer—the layer

of society lying between £2,000 and £300 a year: my
own family was not far from the bottom. You notice
that I define it in terms of money, because that is always
the quickest way of making yourself understood. Nevertheless, the essential point about the English class-system
is that it is *not* entirely explicable in terms of money.
Roughly speaking it is a money-stratification, but it is
also interpenetrated by a sort of shadowy caste-system;
rather like a jerry-built modern bungalow haunted by
medieval ghosts. Hence the fact that the upper-middle
class extends or extended to incomes as low as £300
a year—to incomes, that is, much lower than those of
merely middle-class people with no social pretensions.
Probably there are countries where you can predict a
man's opinions from his income, but it is never quite
safe to do so in England; you have always got to
take his traditions into consideration as well. A naval
officer and his grocer very likely have the same
income, but they are not equivalent persons and they
would only be on the same side in very large issues
such as a war or a general strike—possibly not even
then.

Of course it is obvious now that the upper-middle
class is done for. In every country town in Southern
England, not to mention the dreary wastes of Kensington
and Earl's Court, those who knew it in the days of its
glory, are dying, vaguely embittered by a world which
has not behaved as it ought. I never open one of Kipling's
books or go into one of the huge dull shops which were
once the favourite haunt of the upper-middle class, without thinking " Change and decay in all around I see."
But before the war the upper-middle class, though
already none too prosperous, still felt sure of itself.
Before the war you were either a gentleman or not a

gentleman, and if you were a gentleman you struggled to behave as such, whatever your income might be. Between those with £400 a year and those with £2,000 or even £1,000 a year there was a great gulf fixed, but it was a gulf which those with £400 a year did their best to ignore. Probably the distinguishing mark of the upper-middle class was that its traditions were not to any extent commercial, but mainly military, official, and professional. People in this class owned no land, but they felt that they were landowners in the sight of God and kept up a semi-aristocratic outlook by going into the professions and the fighting services rather than into trade. Small boys used to count the plum stones on their plates and foretell their destiny by chanting " Army, Navy, Church, Medicine, Law "; and even of these " Medicine " was faintly inferior to the others and only put in for the sake of symmetry. To belong to this class when you were at the £400 a year level was a queer business, for it meant that your gentility was almost purely theoretical. You lived, so to speak, at two levels simultaneously. Theoretically you knew all about servants and how to tip them, although in practice you had one or, at most, two resident servants. Theoretically you knew how to wear your clothes and how to order a dinner, although in practice you could never afford to go to a decent tailor or a decent restaurant. Theoretically you knew how to shoot and ride, although in practice you had no horses to ride and not an inch of ground to shoot over. It was this that explained the attraction of India (more recently Kenya, Nigeria, etc.) for the lower-upper-middle class. The people who went there as soldiers and officials did not go there to make money, for a soldier or an official does not make money; they went there because in India, with cheap horses, free shooting, and hordes of black servants, it was so easy to play at being a gentleman.

In the kind of shabby-genteel family that I am talking about there is far more *consciousness* of poverty than in any working-class family above the level of the dole. Rent and clothes and school-bills are an unending nightmare, and every luxury, even a glass of beer, is an unwarrantable extravagance. Practically the whole family income goes in keeping up appearances. It is obvious that people of this kind are in an anomalous position, and one might be tempted to write them off as mere exceptions and therefore unimportant. Actually, however, they are or were fairly numerous. Most clergymen and schoolmasters, for instance, nearly all Anglo-Indian officials, a sprinkling of soldiers and sailors and a fair number of professional men and artists, fall into this category. But the real importance of this class is that they are the shock-absorbers of the bourgeoisie. The real bourgeoisie, those in the £2,000 a year class and over, have their money as a thick layer of padding between themselves and the class they plunder; in so far as they are aware of the Lower Orders at all they are aware of them as employees, servants and tradesmen. But it is quite different for the poor devils lower down who are struggling to live genteel lives on what are virtually working-class incomes. These last are forced into close and, in a sense, intimate contact with the working class, and I suspect it is from them that the traditional upper-class attitude towards " common " people is derived.

And what is this attitude? An attitude of sniggering superiority punctuated by bursts of vicious hatred. Look at any number of *Punch* during the past thirty years. You will find it everywhere taken for granted that a working-class person, as such, is a figure of fun, except at odd moments when he shows signs of being too prosperous, whereupon he ceases to be a figure of fun and becomes a demon. It is no use wasting breath in denouncing this attitude. It is better to consider how it has arisen, and to do that one has got to realise what the working classes look like to those who live among them but have different habits and traditions.

A shabby-genteel family is in much the same position as a family of " poor whites " living in a street where everyone else is a negro. In such circumstances you have got to cling to your gentility because it is the only thing you have; and meanwhile you are hated for your stuck-up-ness and for the accent and manners which stamp you as one of the boss class. I was very young, not much more than six, when I first became aware of class-distinctions. Before that age my chief heroes had generally been working-class people, because they always seemed to do such interesting things, such as being fishermen and blacksmiths and bricklayers. I remember the farm hands on a farm in Cornwall who used to let me ride on the drill when they were sowing turnips and would some-times catch the ewes and milk them to give me a drink; and the workmen building the new house next door, who let me play with the wet mortar and from whom I first learned the word " b—— "; and the plumber up the road with whose children I used to go out bird-nesting. But it was not long before I was forbidden to play with the plumber's children; they were " common " and I was told to keep away from them. This was snobbish, if you like, but it was also necessary, for middle-class people cannot afford to let their children grow up with vulgar accents. So, very early, the working class ceased to be a race of friendly and wonderful beings and became a race of enemies. We realised that they hated

us, but we could never understand why, and naturally
we set it down to pure, vicious malignity. To me in my
early boyhood, to nearly all children of families like
mine, " common " people seemed almost sub-human.
They had coarse faces, hideous accents and gross
manners, they hated everyone who was not like themselves, and if they got half a chance they would insult
you in brutal ways. That was our view of them, and
though it was false it was understandable. For one must
remember that before the war there was much more
overt class-hatred in England than there is now. In those
days you were quite likely to be insulted simply for
looking like a member of the upper classes; nowadays,
on the other hand, you are more likely to be fawned
upon. Anyone over thirty can remember the time when
it was impossible for a well-dressed person to walk
through a slum street without being hooted at. Whole
quarters of big towns were considered unsafe because of
" hooligans " (now almost an extinct type), and the
London gutter-boy everywhere, with his loud voice and
lack of intellectual scruples, could make life a misery for
people who considered it beneath their dignity to answer
back. A recurrent terror of my holidays, when I was
a small boy, was the gangs of " cads " who were liable
to set upon you five or ten to one. In term time, on the
other hand, it was we who were in the majority and the
" cads " who were oppressed; I remember a couple of
savage mass-battles in the cold winter of 1916–17. And
this tradition of open hostility between upper and
lower class had apparently been the same for at least a
century past. A typical joke in *Punch* in the 'sixties is a
picture of a small, nervous-looking gentleman riding
through a slum street and a crowd of street-boys closing
in on him with shouts of " 'Ere comes a swell ! Let's

frighten 'is 'oss!" Just fancy the street boys trying to frighten his horse now ! They would be much likelier to hang round him in vague hopes of a tip. During the past dozen years the English working class have grown servile with a rather horrifying rapidity. It was bound to happen, for the frightful weapon of unemployment has cowed them. Before the war their economic position was comparatively strong, for though there was no dole to fall back upon, there was not much unemployment, and the power of the boss class was not so obvious as it is now. A man did not see ruin staring him in the face every time he cheeked a " toff," and naturally he did cheek a " toff" whenever it seemed safe to do so. G. J. Renier, in his book on Oscar Wilde, points out that the strange, obscene bursts of popular fury which followed the Wilde trial was essentially social in character. The London mob had caught a member of the upper classes on the hop, and they took care to keep him hopping. All this was natural and even proper. If you treat people as the English working class have been treated during the past two centuries, you must expect them to resent it. On the other hand the children of shabby-genteel families could not be blamed if they grew up with a hatred of the working class, typified for them by prowling gangs of " cads."

But there was another and more serious difficulty. Here you come to the real secret of class distinctions in the West—the real reason why a European of bourgeois upbringing, even when he calls himself a Communist, cannot without a hard effort think of a working man as his equal. It is summed up in four frightful words which people nowadays are chary of uttering, but which were bandied about quite freely in my childhood. The words were: *The lower classes smell.*

That was what we were taught—*the lower classes smell*. And here, obviously, you are at an impassable barrier. For no feeling of like or dislike is quite so fundamental as a *physical* feeling. Race-hatred, religious hatred, differences of education, of temperament, of intellect, even differences of moral code, can be got over; but physical repulsion cannot. You can have an affection for a murderer or a sodomite, but you cannot have an affection for a man whose breath stinks—habitually stinks, I mean. However well you may wish him, however much you may admire his mind and character, if his breath stinks he is horrible and in your heart of hearts you will hate him. It may not greatly matter if the average middle-class person is brought up to believe that the working classes are ignorant, lazy, drunken, boorish and dishonest; it is when he is brought up to believe that they are dirty that the harm is done. And in my childhood we *were* brought up to believe that they were dirty. Very early in life you acquired the idea that there was something subtly repulsive about a working-class body; you would not get nearer to it than you could help. You watched a great sweaty navvy walking down the road with his pick over his shoulder; you looked at his discoloured shirt and his corduroy trousers stiff with the dirt of a decade; you thought of those nests and layers of greasy rags below, and, under all, the unwashed body, brown all over (that was how I used to imagine it), with its strong, bacon-like reek. You watched a tramp taking off his boots in a ditch—ugh ! It did not seriously occur to you that the tramp might not enjoy having black feet. And even " lower-class " people whom you knew to be quite clean—servants, for instance—were faintly unappetising. The smell of their sweat, the very texture of their skins, were mysteriously different from yours.

Everyone who has grown up pronouncing his aitches
and in a house with a bathroom and one servant is likely
to have grown up with these feelings; hence the chasmic,
impassable quality of class-distinctions in the West. It
is queer how seldom this is admitted. At the moment I
can think of only one book where it is set forth without
humbug, and that is Mr. Somerset Maugham's *On a
Chinese Screen*. Mr. Maugham describes a high Chinese
official arriving at a wayside inn and blustering and
calling everybody names in order to impress upon them
that he is a supreme dignitary and they are only worms.
Five minutes later, having asserted his dignity in the
way he thinks proper, he is eating his dinner in perfect
amity with the baggage coolies. As an official he feels
that he has got to make his presence felt, but he has no
feeling that the coolies are of different clay from himself. I have observed countless similar scenes in Burma.
Among Mongolians—among all Asiatics, for all I know
—there is a sort of natural equality, an easy intimacy
between man and man, which is simply unthinkable in
the West. Mr. Maugham adds:

" In the West we are divided from our fellows by our sense
of smell. The working man is our master, inclined to rule us
with an iron hand, but it cannot be denied that he stinks:
none can wonder at it, for a bath in the dawn when you have
to hurry to your work before the factory bell rings is no pleasant
thing, nor does heavy labour tend to sweetness; and you do
not change your linen more than you can help when the
week's washing must be done by a sharp-tongued wife. I do not
blame the working man because he stinks, but stink he does.
It makes social intercourse difficult to persons of sensitive
nostril. The matutinal tub divides the classes more effectually
than birth, wealth or education."

Meanwhile, *do* the " lower classes " smell ? Of course, as a whole, they are dirtier than the upper classes. They are bound to be, considering the circumstances in which they live, for even at this late date less than half the houses in England have bathrooms. Besides, the habit of washing yourself all over every day is a very recent one in Europe, and the working classes are generally more conservative than the bourgeoisie. But the English are growing visibly cleaner, and we may hope that in a hundred years they will be almost as clean as the Japanese. It is a pity that those who idealise the working class so often think it necessary to praise every working-class characteristic and therefore to pretend that dirtiness is somehow meritorious in itself. Here, curiously enough, the Socialist and the sentimental democratic Catholic of the type of Chesterton sometimes join hands; both will tell you that dirtiness is healthy and " natural " and cleanliness is a mere fad or at best a luxury.[1] They seem not to see that they are merely giving colour to the notion that working-class people are dirty from choice and not from necessity. Actually, people who have access to a bath will generally use it. But the essential thing is that middle-class people *believe* that the working class are dirty—you see from the passage quoted above that Mr. Maugham himself believes it—and, what is worse, that they are somehow *inherently* dirty. As a child, one of the most dreadful things I could imagine was to drink out of a bottle after a navvy. Once when I was thirteen, I was in a train coming from a market town, and the third-class carriage was packed full of shepherds and pig-men who had been selling their beasts. Somebody

---

[1] According to Chesterton, dirtiness is merely a kind of " discomfort " and therefore ranks as self-mortification. Unfortunately, the discomfort of dirtiness is chiefly suffered by other people. It is not really very uncomfortable to be dirty—not nearly so uncomfortable as having a cold bath on a winter morning.

produced a quart bottle of beer and passed it round; it travelled from mouth to mouth to mouth, everyone taking a swig. I cannot describe the horror I felt as that bottle worked its way towards me. If I drank from it after all those lower-class male mouths I felt certain I should vomit; on the other hand, if they offered it to me I dared not refuse for fear of offending them—you see here how the middle-class squeamishness works both ways. Nowadays, thank God, I have no feelings of that kind. A working-man's body, as such, is no more repulsive to me than a millionaire's. I still don't like drinking out of a cup or bottle after another person—another man, I mean: with women I don't mind—but at least the question of class does not enter. It was rubbing shoulders with the tramps that cured me of it. Tramps are not really very dirty as English people go, but they have the name for being dirty, and when you have shared a bed with a tramp and drunk tea out of the same snuff-tin, you feel that you have seen the worst and the worst has no terrors for you.

I have dwelt on these subjects because they are vitally important. To get rid of class-distinctions you have got to start by understanding how one class appears when seen through the eyes of another. It is useless to say that the middle classes are " snobbish " and leave it at that. You get no further if you do not realise that snobbishness is bound up with a species of idealism. It derives from the early training in which a middle-class child is taught almost simultaneously to wash his neck, to be ready to die for his country, and to despise the " lower classes."

Here I shall be accused of being behind the times, for I was a child before and during the war and it may be claimed that children nowadays are brought up with more enlightened notions. It is probably true that class-feeling is for the moment a very little less bitter than it was. The working class are submissive where they used to be openly hostile, and the post-war manufacture of cheap clothes and the general softening of manners have toned down the surface differences between class and class. But undoubtedly the essential feeling is still there. Every middle-class person has a dormant class-prejudice which needs only a small thing to arouse it; and if he is over forty he probably has a firm conviction that his own class has been sacrificed to the class below. Suggest to the average unthinking person of gentle birth who is struggling to keep up appearances on four or five hundred a year that he is a member of an exploiting parasite class, and he will think you are mad. In perfect sincerity he will point out to you a dozen ways in which he is worse-off than a working man. In his eyes the workers are not a submerged race of slaves, they are a sinister flood creeping upwards to engulf himself and his friends and his family and to sweep all culture and all decency out of existence. Hence that queer watchful anxiety lest the working class shall grow too prosperous. In a number of *Punch* soon after the war, when coal was still fetching high prices, there is a picture of four or five miners with grim, sinister faces riding in a cheap motor-car. A friend they are passing calls out and asks them where they have borrowed it. They answer, " We've bought the thing ! " This, you see, is " good enough for *Punch* "; for miners to buy a motor-car, even one car between four or five of them, is a monstrosity, a sort of crime against nature. That was the attitude of a dozen years ago, and I see no evidence of any fundamental change. The notion that the working class have been absurdly pampered, hopelessly demoralised by doles, old age pensions, free education, etc., is still widely held; it has merely been a little shaken, perhaps, by the recent recognition that unemployment does exist. For quantities of middle-class people, probably for a large majority of those over fifty, the typical working man still rides to the Labour Exchange on a motor-bike and keeps coal in his bathtub: " And, if you'll believe it, my dear, they actually *get married* on the dole ! "

The reason why class-hatred seems to be diminishing is that nowadays it tends not to get into print, partly owing to the mealy-mouthed habits of our time, partly because newspapers and even books now have to appeal to a working-class public. As a rule you can best study it in private conversations. But if you want some printed examples, it is worth having a look at the *obiter dicta* of the late Professor Saintsbury. Saintsbury was a very learned man and along certain lines a judicious literary critic, but when he talked of political or economic matters he only differed from the rest of his class by the fact that he was too thick-skinned and had been born too early to see any reason for pretending to common decency. According to Saintsbury, unemployment insurance was simply " contributing to the support of lazy ne'er-do-weels," and the whole trade union movement was no more than a kind of organised mendicancy:

" ' Pauper ' is almost actionable now, is it not, when used as a word ? though to *be* paupers, in the sense of being wholly or partly supported at the expense of other people, is the ardent, and to a considerable extent achieved, aspiration of a large proportion of our population, and of an entire political party."

(*Second Scrap Book.*)

It is to be noticed, however, that Saintsbury recognises that unemployment is bound to exist, and, in fact, thinks

that it ought to exist, so long as the unemployed are
made to suffer as much as possible:

> " Is not ' casual ' labour the very secret and safety-valve of
> a safe and sound labour-system generally ?
> " . . . In a complicated industrial and commercial state con-
> stant employment at regular wages is impossible; while dole-
> supported unemployment, at anything like the wages of
> employment, is demoralising to begin with and ruinous at its
> more or less quickly arriving end."
>
> *(Last Scrap Book.)*

What exactly is to happen to the " casual labourers "
when no casual labour happens to be available is not
made clear. Presumably (Saintsbury speaks approvingly
of " good Poor Laws ") they are to go into the workhouse or sleep in the streets. As to the notion that every
human being ought as a matter of course to have the
chance of earning at least a tolerable livelihood, Saintsbury dismisses it with contempt:

> " Even the ' right to live ' . . . extends no further than the
> right to protection against murder. Charity certainly will,
> morality possibly may, and public utility perhaps ought to add
> to this protection supererogatory provision for continuance of
> life; but it is questionable whether strict justice demands it.
> " As for the insane doctrine that being born in a country
> gives some right to the possession of the soil of that country,
> it hardly requires notice."
>
> *(Last Scrap Book.)*

It is worth reflecting for a moment upon the beautiful
implications of this last passage. The interest of passages
like these (and they are scattered all through Saintsbury's work) lies in their having been printed at all.
Most people are a little shy of putting that kind of thing
on paper. But what Saintsbury is saying here is what any

little worm with a fairly safe five hundred a year *thinks*, and therefore in a way one must admire him for saying it. It takes a lot of guts to be *openly* such a skunk as that.

This is the outlook of a confessed reactionary. But how about the middle-class person whose views are not reactionary but " advanced " ? Beneath his revolutionary mask, is he really so different from the other ?

A middle-class person embraces Socialism and perhaps even joins the Communist Party. How much real difference does it make ? Obviously, living within the framework of capitalist society, he has got to go on earning his living, and one cannot blame him if he clings to his bourgeois economic status. But is there any change in his tastes, his habits, his manners, his imaginative background—his " ideology," in Communist jargon ? Is there *any* change in him except that he now votes Labour, or, when possible, Communist at the elections ? It is noticeable that he still habitually associates with his own class ; he is vastly more at home with a member of his own class, who thinks him a dangerous Bolshie, than with a member of the working class who supposedly agrees with him ; his tastes in food, wine, clothes, books, pictures, music, ballet, are still recognisably bourgeois tastes ; most significant of all, he invariably marries into his own class. Look at any bourgeois Socialist. Look at Comrade X, member of the C.P.G.B. and author of *Marxism for Infants*. Comrade X, it so happens, is an old Etonian. He would be ready to die on the barricades, in theory anyway, but you notice that he still leaves his bottom waistcoat button undone. He idealises the proletariat, but it is remarkable how little his habits resemble theirs. Perhaps once, out of sheer bravado, he has smoked a cigar with the band on, but it would be almost physically impossible for him to put pieces of cheese into his mouth on the point of his knife, or to sit indoors with his cap on, or even to drink his tea out of the saucer. Perhaps table-manners are not a bad test of sincerity. I have known numbers of bourgeois Socialists, I have listened by the hour to their tirades against their own class, and yet never, not even once, have I met one who had picked up proletarian table-manners. Yet, after all, why not? Why should a man who thinks all virtue resides in the proletariat still take such pains to drink his soup silently? It can only be because in his heart he feels that proletarian manners are disgusting. So you see he is still responding to the training of his childhood, when he was taught to hate, fear, and despise the working class.

CHAPTER IX

WHEN I WAS FOURTEEN OR FIFTEEN I was an odious little snob, but no worse than other boys of my own age and class. I suppose there is no place in the world where snobbery is quite so ever-present or where it is cultivated in such refined and subtle forms as in an English public school. Here at least one cannot say that English " education " fails to do its job. You forget your Latin and Greek within a few months of leaving school—I studied Greek for eight or ten years, and now, at thirty-three, I cannot even repeat the Greek alphabet—but your snobbishness, unless you persistently root it out like the bindweed it is, sticks by you till your grave.

At school I was in a difficult position, for I was among boys who, for the most part, were much richer than myself, and I only went to an expensive public school because I happened to win a scholarship. This is the common experience of boys of the lower-upper-middle class, the sons of clergymen, Anglo-Indian officials, etc., and the effects it had on me were probably the usual ones. On the one hand it made me cling tighter than ever to my gentility; on the other hand it filled me with resentment against the boys whose parents were richer than mine and who took care to let me know it. I despised anyone who was not describable as a " gentleman," but also I hated the hoggishly rich, especially those who had grown rich too recently. The correct and elegant thing, I felt, was to be of gentle birth but to have no money. This is part of the *credo* of the lower-upper-middle class. It has a romantic, Jacobite-in-exile feeling about it which is very comforting.

But those years, during and just after the war, were a queer time to be at school, for England was nearer revolution than she has been since or had been for a century earlier. Throughout almost the whole nation there was running a wave of revolutionary feeling which has since been reversed and forgotten, but which has left various deposits of sediment behind. Essentially, though of course one could not then see it in perspective, it was a revolt of youth against age, resulting directly from the war. In the war the young had been sacrificed and the old had behaved in a way which, even at this distance of time, is horrible to contemplate; they had been sternly patriotic in safe places while their sons went down like swathes of hay before the German machine guns. Moreover, the war had been conducted mainly by old men and had been conducted with supreme incompetence. By 1918 everyone under forty was in a bad temper with his elders, and the mood of anti-militarism which followed naturally upon the fighting was extended into a general revolt against orthodoxy and authority. At that time there was, among the young, a curious cult of hatred of " old men." The dominance of " old men " was held to be responsible for every evil known to humanity, and every accepted institution from Scott's novels to the House of Lords was derided merely because " old men " were in favour of it. For several years it was all the fashion to be a " Bolshie," as people then called it. England was full of half-baked antinomian opinions. Pacifism, internationalism, humanitarianism of all kinds, feminism, free love, divorce-reform, atheism, birth-control—things like these were getting a better hearing than they would get in normal times. And of course the revolutionary mood extended to those who had been too young to fight, even to public schoolboys. At that time we all thought of ourselves as enlightened creatures of a new age, casting off the orthodoxy that had been forced upon us by those detested " old men." We retained, basically, the snobbish outlook of our class, we took it for granted that we should continue to draw our dividends or tumble into soft jobs, but also it seemed natural to us to be " agin the government." We derided the O.T.C., the Christian religion, and perhaps even compulsory games and the Royal Family, and we did not realise that we were merely taking part in a world-wide gesture of distaste for war. Two incidents stick in my mind as examples of the queer revolutionary feeling of that time. One day the master who taught us English set us a kind of general knowledge paper of which one of the questions was, " Whom do you consider the ten greatest men now living ? " Of sixteen boys in the class (our average age was about seventeen) fifteen included Lenin in their list. This was at a snobbish expensive public school, and the date was 1920, when the horrors of the Russian Revolution were still fresh in everyone's mind. Also there were the so-called peace celebrations in 1919. Our elders had decided for us that we should celebrate peace in the traditional manner by whooping over the fallen foe. We were to march into the school-yard, carrying torches, and sing jingo songs of the type of " Rule Britannia." The boys—to their honour, I think—guyed the whole proceeding and sang blasphemous and seditious words to the tunes provided. I doubt whether things would happen in quite that manner now. Certainly the public schoolboys I meet nowadays, even the intelligent ones, are much more right-wing in their opinions than I and my contemporaries were fifteen years ago.

Hence, at the age of seventeen or eighteen, I was both a snob and a revolutionary. I was against all authority. I had read and re-read the entire published works of Shaw, Wells, and Galsworthy (at that time still regarded as dangerously " advanced " writers), and I loosely described myself as a Socialist. But I had not much grasp of what Socialism meant, and no notion that the working class were human beings. At a distance, and through the medium of books—Jack London's *The People of the Abyss*, for instance—I could agonise over their sufferings, but I still hated them and despised them when I came anywhere near them. I was still revolted by their accents and infuriated by their habitual rudeness. One must remember that just then, immediately after the war, the English working class were in a fighting mood. That was the period of the great coal strikes, when a miner was thought of as a fiend incarnate and old ladies looked under their beds every night lest Robert Smillie should be concealed there. All through the war and for a little time afterwards there had been high wages and abundant employment; things were now returning to something worse than normal, and naturally the working class resisted. The men who had fought had been lured into the army by gaudy promises, and now they were coming home to a world where there were no jobs and not even any houses. Moreover, they had been at war and were coming home with the soldier's attitude to life, which is fundamentally, in spite of discipline, a lawless attitude. There was a turbulent feeling in the air. To that time belongs the song with the memorable refrain:

There's nothing sure but
The rich get richer and the poor get children;
In the mean time,
In between time,
Ain't we got fun?

People had not yet settled down to a lifetime of unemployment mitigated by endless cups of tea. They still
vaguely expected the Utopia for which they had fought,
and even more than before they were openly hostile to
the aitch-pronouncing class. So to the shock-absorbers
of the bourgeoisie, such as myself, " common people "
still appeared brutal and repulsive. Looking back upon
that period, I seem to have spent half the time in denouncing the capitalist system and the other half in
raging over the insolence of bus-conductors.

When I was not yet twenty I went to Burma, in the
Indian Imperial Police. In an " outpost of Empire "
like Burma the class-question appeared at first sight to
have been shelved. There was no obvious class-friction
here, because the all-important thing was not whether
you had been to one of the right schools but whether
your skin was technically white. As a matter of fact most
of the white men in Burma were not of the type who in
England would be called " gentlemen," but except for
the common soldiers and a few nondescripts they lived
lives appropriate to " gentlemen "—had servants, that
is, and called their evening meal " dinner "—and
officially they were regarded as being all of the same
class. They were " white men," in contradistinction to
the other and inferior class, the " natives." But one did
not feel towards the " natives " as one felt towards the
" lower classes " at home. The essential point was that
the " natives," at any rate the Burmese, were not felt
to be physically repulsive. One looked down on them as

" natives," but one was quite ready to be physically
intimate with them; and this, I noticed, was the case
even with white men who had the most vicious colour-
prejudice. When you have a lot of servants you soon get
into lazy habits, and I habitually allowed myself, for
instance, to be dressed and undressed by my Burmese
boy. This was because he was a Burman and undisgust-
ing; I could not have endured to let an English man-
servant handle me in that intimate manner. I felt towards a Burman almost as I felt towards a woman.
Like most other races, the Burmese have a distinctive
smell—I cannot describe it: it is a smell that makes one's
teeth tingle—but this smell never disgusted me. (Incidentally, orientals say that *we* smell. The Chinese, I
believe, say that a white man smells like a corpse. The
Burmese say the same—though no Burman was ever
rude enough to say so to me.) And in a way my attitude
was defensible, for if one faces facts one must admit that
most Mongolians have much nicer bodies than most
white men. Compare the firm-knit silken skin of the
Burman, which does not wrinkle at all till he is past forty,
and then merely withers up like a piece of dry leather,
with the coarse-grained, flabby, sagging skin of the
white man. The white man has lank ugly hair growing
down his legs and the backs of his arms and in an ugly
patch on his chest. The Burman has only a tuft or two
of stiff black hair at the appropriate places; for the rest
he is quite hairless and is usually beardless as well. The
white man almost always goes bald, the Burman seldom
or never. The Burman's teeth are perfect, though
generally discoloured by betel juice, the white man's
teeth invariably decay. The white man is generally ill-
shaped, and when he grows fat he bulges in improbable
places; the Mongol has beautiful bones and in old age

he is almost as shapely as in youth. Admittedly the white races throw up a few individuals who for a few years are supremely beautiful; but on the whole, say what you will, they are far less comely than orientals. But it was not of this that I was thinking when I found the English "lower classes" so much more repellent than Burmese "natives." I was still thinking in terms of my early-acquired class-prejudice. When I was not much past twenty I was attached for a short time to a British regiment. Of course I admired and liked the private soldiers as any youth of twenty would admire and like hefty, cheery youths five years older than himself with the medals of the Great War on their chests. And yet, after all, they faintly repelled me; they were "common people" and I did not care to be too close to them. In the hot mornings when the company marched down the road, myself in the rear with one of the junior subalterns, the steam of those hundred sweating bodies in front made my stomach turn. And this, you observe, was pure prejudice. For a soldier is probably as inoffensive, physically, as it is possible for a male white person to be. He is generally young, he is nearly always healthy from fresh air and exercise, and a rigorous discipline compels him to be clean. But I could not see it like that. All I knew was that it was *lower-class* sweat that I was smelling, and the thought of it made me sick.

When later on I got rid of my class-prejudice, or part of it, it was in a roundabout way and by a process that took several years. The thing that changed my attitude to the class-issue was something only indirectly connected with it—something almost irrelevant.

I was in the Indian Police five years, and by the end of that time I hated the imperialism I was serving with a bitterness which I probably cannot make clear. In the free air of England that kind of thing is not fully intelligible. In order to hate imperialism you have got to be part of it. Seen from the outside the British rule in India appears—indeed, it *is*—benevolent and even necessary; and so no doubt are the French rule in Morocco and the Dutch rule in Borneo, for people usually govern foreigners better than they govern themselves. But it is not possible to be part of such a system without recognising it as an unjustifiable tyranny. Even the thickest-skinned Anglo-Indian is aware of this. Every " native " face he sees in the street brings home to him his monstrous intrusion. And the majority of Anglo-Indians, intermittently at least, are not nearly so complacent about their position as people in England believe. From the most unexpected people, from gin-pickled old scoundrels high up in the Government service, I have heard some such remark as: " Of course we've no right in this blasted country at all. Only now we're here for God's sake let's stay here." The truth is that no modern man, in his heart of hearts, believes that it is right to invade a foreign country and hold the population down by force. Foreign oppression is a much more obvious, understandable evil than economic oppression. Thus in England we tamely admit to being robbed in order to keep half a million worthless idlers in luxury, but we would fight to the last man sooner than be ruled by Chinamen; similarly, people who live on unearned dividends without a single qualm of conscience, see clearly enough that it is wrong to go and lord it in a foreign country where you are not wanted. The result is that every Anglo-Indian is haunted by a sense of guilt which he usually conceals as best he can, because there is no freedom of speech, and merely to be overheard making a seditious remark may damage his career. All over India there are Englishmen who secretly loathe the system of which they are part; and just occasionally, when they are quite certain of being in the right company, their hidden bitterness overflows. I remember a night I spent on the train with a man in the Educational Service, a stranger to myself whose name I never discovered. It was too hot to sleep and we spent the night in talking. Half an hour's cautious questioning decided each of us that the other was " safe "; and then for hours, while the train jolted slowly through the pitch-black night, sitting up in our bunks with bottles of beer handy, we damned the British Empire—damned it from the inside, intelligently and intimately. It did us both good. But we had been speaking forbidden things, and in the haggard morning light when the train crawled into Mandalay, we parted as guiltily as any adulterous couple.

So far as my observation goes nearly all Anglo-Indian officials have moments when their conscience troubles them. The exceptions are men who are doing something which is demonstrably useful and would still have to be done whether the British were in India or not: forest officers, for instance, and doctors and engineers. But I was in the police, which is to say that I was part of the actual machinery of despotism. Moreover, in the police you see the dirty work of Empire at close quarters, and there is an appreciable difference between doing dirty work and merely profiting by it. Most people approve of capital punishment, but most people wouldn't do the hangman's job. Even the other Europeans in Burma slightly looked down on the police because of the brutal work they had to do. I remember once when I was inspecting a police station, an American missionary whom I knew fairly well came in for some purpose or other. Like most Nonconformist missionaries he was a complete ass but quite a good fellow. One of my native sub-inspectors was bullying a suspect (I described this scene in *Burmese Days*). The American watched it, and then turning to me said thoughtfully, " I wouldn't care to have your job." It made me horribly ashamed. So *that* was the kind of job I had ! Even an ass of an American missionary, a teetotal cock-virgin from the Middle West, had the right to look down on me and pity me ! But I should have felt the same shame even if there had been no one to bring it home to me. I had begun to have an indescribable loathing of the whole machinery of so-called justice. Say what you will, our criminal law (far more humane, by the way, in India than in England) is a horrible thing. It needs very insensitive people to administer it. The wretched prisoners squatting in the reeking cages of the lock-ups, the grey cowed faces of the long-term convicts, the scarred buttocks of the men who had been flogged with bamboos, the women and children howling when their menfolk were led away under arrest—things like these are beyond bearing when you are in any way directly responsible for them. I watched a man hanged once; it seemed to me worse than a thousand murders. I never went into a jail without feeling (most visitors to jails feel the same) that my place was on the other side of the bars. I thought then—I think now, for that matter—that the worst criminal who ever walked is morally superior to a hanging judge. But of course I had to keep these notions to myself, because of the almost utter silence that is imposed on every Englishman in the East. In the end I worked out an anarchistic theory that all government is evil, that the punishment always does more harm than the crime and that people can be trusted to behave decently if only you will let them alone. This of course was sentimental nonsense. I see now as I did not see then, that it is always necessary to protect peaceful people from violence. In any state of society where crime can be profitable you have got to have a harsh criminal law and administer it ruthlessly; the alternative is Al Capone. But the feeling that punishment is evil arises inescapably in those who have to administer it. I should expect to find that even in England many policemen, judges, prison warders, and the like are haunted by a secret horror of what they do. But in Burma it was a double oppression that we were committing. Not only were we hanging people and putting them in jail and so forth; we were doing it in the capacity of unwanted foreign invaders. The Burmese themselves never really recognised our jurisdiction. The thief whom we put in prison did not think of himself as a criminal justly punished, he thought of himself as the victim of a foreign conqueror. The thing that was done to him was merely a wanton meaningless cruelty. His face, behind the stout teak bars of the lock-up and the iron bars of the jail, said so clearly. And unfortunately I had not trained myself to be indifferent to the expression of the human face.

When I came home on leave in 1927 I was already half determined to throw up my job, and one sniff of English air decided me. I was not going back to be a part of that evil despotism. But I wanted much more than merely to escape from my job. For five years I had been part of an oppressive system, and it had left me with a bad conscience. Innumerable remembered faces—faces of prisoners in the dock, of men waiting in the con- demned cells, of subordinates I had bullied and aged peasants I had snubbed, of servants and coolies I had hit with my fist in moments of rage (nearly everyone does these things in the East, at any rate occasionally: orientals can be very provoking)—haunted me intolerably. I was conscious of an immense weight of guilt that I had got to expiate. I suppose that sounds exaggerated; but if you do for five years a job that you thoroughly disapprove of, you will probably feel the same. I had reduced everything to the simple theory that the oppressed are always right and the oppressors are always wrong: a mistaken theory, but the natural result of being one of the oppressors yourself. I felt that I had got to escape not merely from imperialism but from every form of man's dominion over man. I wanted to submerge myself, to get right down among the oppressed, to be one of them and on their side against their tyrants. And, chiefly because I had had to think everything out in solitude, I had carried my hatred of oppression to extraordinary lengths. At that time failure seemed to me to be the only virtue. Every suspicion of self-advancement, even to " succeed " in life to the extent of making a few hundreds a year, seemed to me spiritually ugly, a species of bullying.

It was in this way that my thoughts turned towards the English working class. It was the first time that I had ever been really aware of the working class, and to begin with it was only because they supplied an analogy. They were the symbolic victims of injustice, playing the same part in England as the Burmese played in Burma. In Burma the issue had been quite simple. The whites were up and the blacks were down, and therefore as a matter of course one's sympathy was with the blacks. I now realised that there was no need to go as far as Burma to find tyranny and exploitation. Here in England, down under one's feet, were the submerged working class, suffering miseries which in their different way were as bad as any an oriental ever knows. The word "unemployment" was on everyone's lips. That was more or less new to me, after Burma, but the drivel which the middle classes were still talking ("These unemployed are all unemployables," etc., etc.) failed to deceive me. I often wonder whether that kind of stuff deceives even the fools who utter it. On the other hand I had at that time no interest in Socialism or any other economic theory. It seemed to me then—it sometimes seems to me now, for that matter—that economic injustice will stop the moment we want it to stop, and no sooner, and if we genuinely want it to stop the method adopted hardly matters.

But I knew nothing about working-class conditions. I had read the unemployment figures but I had no notion of what they implied; above all, I did not know the essential fact that "respectable" poverty is always the worst. The frightful doom of a decent working man suddenly thrown on the streets after a lifetime of steady work, his agonised struggles against economic laws which he does not understand, the disintegration of families, the corroding sense of shame—all this was outside the range of my experience. When I thought of poverty I thought of it in terms of brute starvation. Therefore my mind turned immediately towards the extreme cases, the social outcasts: tramps, beggars, criminals, prostitutes. These were "the lowest of the low," and these were the people with whom I wanted to get in contact. What I profoundly wanted, at that time, was to find some way of getting out of the respectable world altogether. I meditated upon it a great deal, I even planned parts of it in detail; how one could sell everything, give everything away, change one's name and start out with no money and nothing but the clothes one stood up in. But in real life nobody ever does that kind of thing; apart from the relatives and friends who have to be considered, it is doubtful whether an educated man *could* do it if there were any other course open to him. But at least I could go among these people, see what their lives were like and feel myself temporarily part of their world. Once I had been among them and accepted by them, I should have touched bottom, and—this is what I felt: I was aware even then that it was irrational—part of my guilt would drop from me.

I thought it over and decided what I would do. I would go suitably disguised to Limehouse and White-chapel and such places and sleep in common lodging-houses and pal up with dock labourers, street hawkers, derelict people, beggars, and, if possible, criminals. And I would find out about tramps and how you got in touch with them and what was the proper procedure for entering the casual ward; and then, when I felt that I knew the ropes well enough, I would go on the road myself.

At the start it was not easy. It meant masquerading and I have no talent for acting. I cannot, for instance, disguise my accent, at any rate not for more than a very few minutes. I imagined—notice the frightful class-consciousness of the Englishman—that I should be spotted as a " gentleman " the moment I opened my mouth; so I had a hard luck story ready in case I should be questioned. I got hold of the right kind of clothes and dirtied them in appropriate places. I am a difficult person to disguise, being abnormally tall, but I did at least know what a tramp looks like. (How few people do know this, by the way ! Look at any picture of a tramp in *Punch*. They are always twenty years out of date.) One evening, having made ready at a friend's house, I set out and wandered eastward till I landed up at a common lodging-house in Lime-house Causeway. It was a dark, dirty-looking place. I knew it was a common lodging-house by the sign "Good Beds for Single Men" in the window. Heavens, how I had to screw up my courage before I went in! It seems ridiculous now. But you see I was still half afraid of the working class. I wanted to get in touch with them, I even wanted to become one of them, but I still thought of them as alien and dangerous; going into the dark doorway of that common lodging-house seemed to me like going down into some dreadful subterranean place —a sewer full of rats, for instance. I went in fully expecting a fight. The people would spot that I was not one of themselves and immediately infer that I had come to spy on them; and then they would set upon me and throw me out—that was what I expected. I felt that I had got to do it, but I did not enjoy the prospect.

Inside the door a man in shirt-sleeves appeared from somewhere or other. This was the "deputy," and I told him that I wanted a bed for the night. My accent did not make him stare, I noticed; he merely demanded ninepence and then showed me the way to a frowsy firelit kitchen underground. There were stevedores and navvies and a few sailors sitting about and playing draughts and drinking tea. They barely glanced at me as I entered. But this was Saturday night and a hefty young stevedore was drunk and was reeling about the room. He turned, saw me and lurched towards me with broad red face thrust out and a dangerous-looking fishy gleam in his eyes. I stiffened myself. So the fight was coming already! The next moment the stevedore collapsed on my chest and flung his arms round my neck. " 'Ave a cup of tea, chum ! " he cried tearfully; " 'ave a cup of tea ! "

I had a cup of tea. It was a kind of baptism. After that my fears vanished. Nobody questioned me, nobody showed offensive curiosity; everybody was polite and gentle and took me utterly for granted. I stayed two or three days in that common lodging-house, and a few weeks later, having picked up a certain amount of information about the habits of destitute people, I went on the road for the first time.

I have described all this in *Down and Out in Paris and London* (nearly all the incidents described there actually happened, though they have been rearranged) and I do not want to repeat it. Later I went on the road for much longer periods, sometimes from choice, sometimes from necessity. I have lived in common lodging-houses for months together. But it is that first expedition that sticks most vividly in my mind, because of the strangeness of it—the strangeness of being at last down there among " the lowest of the low," and on terms of utter equality with working-class people. A tramp, it is true, is not a typical working-class person; still, when you are among tramps you are at any rate merged in one section—one sub-caste—of the working class, a thing which so far as I know can happen to you in no other way. For several days I wandered through the northern outskirts of London with an Irish tramp. I was his mate, temporarily. We shared the same cell at night, and he told me the history of his life and I told him a fictitious history of mine, and we took it in turns to beg at likely-looking houses and divided up the proceeds. I was very happy. Here I was, among " the lowest of the low," at the bedrock of the Western world ! The class-bar was down, or seemed to be down. And down there in the squalid and, as a matter of fact, horribly boring sub-world of the tramp I had a feeling of release, of adventure, which seems absurd when I look back, but which was sufficiently vivid at the time.

CHAPTER X

BUT UNFORTUNATELY you do not solve the class problem by making friends with tramps. At most you get rid of some of your own class-prejudice by doing so.

Tramps, beggars, criminals and social outcasts generally are very exceptional beings and no more typical of the working class as a whole than, say, the literary intelligentsia are typical of the bourgeoisie. It is quite easy to be on terms of intimacy with a foreign " intellectual," but it is not at all easy to be on terms of intimacy with an ordinary respectable foreigner of the middle class. How many Englishmen have seen the inside of an ordinary French bourgeois family, for instance ? Probably it would be quite impossible to do so, short of marrying into it. And it is rather similar with the English working class. Nothing is easier than to be bosom pals with a pickpocket, if you know where to look for him; but it is very difficult to be bosom pals with a bricklayer.

But why is it so easy to be on equal terms with social outcasts ? People have often said to me, " Surely when you are with the tramps they don't really accept you as one of themselves ? Surely they notice that you are different—notice the difference of accent ? " etc., etc. As a matter of fact, a fair proportion of tramps, well over a quarter I should say, notice nothing of the kind. To begin with, many people have no ear for accent and judge you entirely by your clothes. I was often struck by this fact when I was begging at back doors. Some people were obviously surprised by my "educated" accent, others completely failed to notice it; I was dirty and ragged and that was all they saw. Again, tramps come from all parts of the British Isles and the variation in English accents is enormous. A tramp is used to hearing all kinds of accents among his mates, some of them so strange to him that he can hardly understand them, and a man from, say, Cardiff or Durham or Dublin does not necessarily know which of the south English accents is an " educated " one. In any case men with " educated " accents, though rare among tramps, are not unknown. But even when tramps are aware that you are of different origin from themselves, it does not necessarily alter their attitude. From their point of view all that matters is that you, like themselves, are " on the bum." And in that world it is not done to ask too many questions. You can tell people the history of your life if you choose, and most tramps do so on the smallest provocation, but you are under no compulsion to tell it and whatever story you tell will be accepted without question. Even a bishop could be at home among tramps if he wore the right clothes; and even if they knew he was a bishop it might not make any difference, provided that they also knew or believed that he was genuinely destitute. Once you are in that world and seemingly *of* it, it hardly matters what you have been in the past. It is a sort of world-within-a-world where everyone is equal, a small squalid democracy—perhaps the nearest thing to a democracy that exists in England.

But when you come to the normal working class the position is totally different. To begin with, there is no short cut into their midst. You can become a tramp simply by putting on the right clothes and going to the nearest casual ward, but you can't become a navvy or a coal-miner. You couldn't get a job as a navvy or a coal-miner even if you were equal to the work. Via Socialist politics you can get in touch with the working-class intelligentsia, but they are hardly more typical than tramps or burglars. For the rest you can only mingle with the working class by staying in their houses as a lodger, which always has a dangerous resemblance to "slumming." For some months I lived entirely in coal-miners' houses. I ate my meals with the family, I washed at the kitchen sink, I shared bedrooms with miners, drank beer with them, played darts with them, talked to them by the hour together. But though I was among them, and I hope and trust they did not find me a nuisance, I was not one of them, and they knew it even better than I did. However much you like them, however interesting you find their conversation, there is always that accursed itch of class-difference, like the pea under the princess's mattress. It is not a question of dislike or distaste, only of *difference*, but it is enough to make real intimacy impossible. Even with miners who described themselves as Communists I found that it needed tactful manœuvrings to prevent them from calling me " sir "; and all of them, except in moments of great animation, softened their northern accents for my benefit. I liked them and hoped they liked me; but I went among them as a foreigner, and both of us were aware of it. Which ever way you turn this curse of class-difference confronts you like a wall of stone. Or rather it is not so much like a stone wall as the plate-glass pane of an aquarium; it is so easy to pretend that it isn't there, and so impossible to get through it.

Unfortunately it is nowadays the fashion to pretend

that the glass is penetrable. Of course everyone knows
that class-prejudice exists, but at the same time everyone
claims that *he*, in some mysterious way, is exempt from
it. Snobbishness is one of those vices which we can
discern in everyone else but never in ourselves. Not only
the *croyant et pratiquant* Socialist, but every " intellectual "
takes it as a matter of course that *he* at least is outside
the class-racket; *he*, unlike his neighbours, can see
through the absurdity of wealth, ranks, titles, etc., etc.
" I'm not a snob " is nowadays a kind of universal
credo. Who is there who has not jeered at the House of
Lords, the military caste, the Royal Family, the public
schools, the huntin' and shootin' people, the old ladies
in Cheltenham boarding-houses, the horrors of
" county " society and the social hierarchy generally ?
To do so has become an automatic gesture. You notice
this particularly in novels. Every novelist of serious pretensions adopts an ironic attitude towards his upper-
class characters. Indeed when a novelist has to put a
definitely upper-class person—a duke or a baronet or
whatnot—into one of his stories he guys him more or
less instinctively. There is an important subsidiary cause
of this in the poverty of the modern upper-class dialect.
The speech of " educated " people is now so lifeless and
characterless that a novelist can do nothing with it. By
far the easiest way of making it amusing is to burlesque
it, which means pretending that every upper-class person is an ineffectual ass. The trick is imitated from
novelist to novelist, and in the end becomes almost
a reflex action.

And yet all the while, at the bottom of his heart,
everyone knows that this is humbug. We all rail against
class-distinctions, but very few people seriously want to
abolish them. Here you come upon the important fact

that every revolutionary opinion draws part of its strength from a secret conviction that nothing can be changed.

If you want a good illustration of this, it is worth studying the novels and plays of John Galsworthy, keeping one eye on their chronology. Galsworthy is a very fine specimen of the thin-skinned, tear-in-the-eye, pre-war humanitarian. He starts out with a morbid pity-complex which extends even to thinking that every married woman is an angel chained to a satyr. He is in a perpetual quiver of indignation over the sufferings of overworked clerks, of under-paid farm hands, of fallen women, of criminals, of prostitutes, of animals. The world, as he sees it in his earlier books (*The Man of Property*, *Justice*, etc.), is divided into oppressors and oppressed, with the oppressors sitting on top like some monstrous stone idol which all the dynamite in the world cannot overthrow. But is it so certain that he really wants it overthrown? On the contrary, in his fight against an immovable tyranny he is upheld by the consciousness that it *is* immovable. When things happen unexpectedly and the world-order which he has known begins to crumble, he feels somewhat differently about it. So, having set out to be the champion of the underdog against tyranny and injustice, he ends by advocating (*vide The Silver Spoon*) that the English working class, to cure their economic ills, shall be deported to the colonies like batches of cattle. If he had lived ten years longer he would quite probably have arrived at some genteel version of Fascism. This is the inevitable fate of the sentimentalist. All his opinions change into their opposites at the first brush of reality.

The same streak of soggy half-baked insincerity runs through all " advanced " opinion. Take the question of

imperialism, for instance. Every left-wing " intellectual "
is, as a matter of course, an anti-imperialist. He claims
to be outside the empire-racket as automatically and
self-righteously as he claims to be outside the class-
racket. Even the right-wing " intellectual," who is not
definitely in revolt against British imperialism, pretends
to regard it with a sort of amused detachment. It is so
easy to be witty about the British Empire. The White
Man's Burden and " Rule Britannia " and Kipling's
novels and Anglo-Indian bores—who could even mention such things without a snigger ? And is there any
cultured person who has not at least once in his life
made a joke about that old Indian havildar who said
that if the British left India there would not be a rupee
or a virgin left between Peshawar and Delhi (or
wherever it was) ? That is the attitude of the typical
left-winger towards imperialism, and a thoroughly
flabby, boneless attitude it is. For in the last resort, the
only important question is, Do you want the British
Empire to hold together or do you want it to disintegrate ? And at the bottom of his heart no Englishman, least of all the kind of person who is witty about
Anglo-Indian colonels, does want it to disintegrate. For,
apart from any other consideration, the high standard
of life we enjoy in England depends upon our keeping
a tight hold on the Empire, particularly the tropical
portions of it such as India and Africa. Under the
capitalist system, in order that England may live in
comparative comfort, a hundred million Indians must
live on the verge of starvation—an evil state of affairs,
but you acquiesce in it every time you step into a taxi
or eat a plate of strawberries and cream. The alternative
is to throw the Empire overboard and reduce England
to a cold and unimportant little island where we should

all have to work very hard and live mainly on herrings and potatoes. That is the very last thing that any left-winger wants. Yet the left-winger continues to feel that he has no moral responsibility for imperialism. He is perfectly ready to accept the products of Empire and to save his soul by sneering at the people who hold the Empire together.

It is at this point that one begins to grasp the unreality of most people's attitude towards the class question. So long as it is merely a question of ameliorating the worker's lot, every decent person is agreed. Take a coal-miner, for example. Everyone, barring fools and scoundrels, would *like* to see the miner better off. If, for instance, the miner could ride to the coal face in a comfortable trolley instead of crawling on his hands and knees, if he could work a three-hour shift instead of seven and a half hours, if he could live in a decent house with five bedrooms and a bathroom and have ten pounds a week wages—splendid! Moreover, anyone who uses his brain knows perfectly well that this is within the range of possibility. The world, potentially at least, is immensely rich; develop it as it might be developed, and we could all live like princes, supposing that we wanted to. And to a very superficial glance the social side of the question looks equally simple. In a sense it is true that almost everyone would like to see class-distinctions abolished. Obviously this perpetual uneasiness between man and man, from which we suffer in modern England, is a curse and a nuisance. Hence the temptation to believe that it can be shouted out of existence with a few scoutmasterish bellows of good-will. Stop calling me " sir," you chaps ! Surely we're all men ? Let's pal up and get our shoulders to the wheel and remember that we're all equal, and what the devil does it matter if I know what kind of ties to wear and you don't, and I drink my soup comparatively quietly and you drink yours with the noise of water going down a waste-pipe—and so on and so on and so on; all of it the most pernicious rubbish, but quite alluring when it is suitably expressed.

But unfortunately you get no further by merely wishing class-distinctions away. More exactly, it *is* necessary to wish them away, but your wish has no efficacy unless you grasp what it involves. The fact that has got to be faced is that to abolish class-distinctions means abolishing a part of yourself. Here am I, a typical member of the middle class. It is easy for me to say that I want to get rid of class-distinctions, but nearly everything I think and do is a result of class-distinctions. All my notions—notions of good and evil, of pleasant and unpleasant, of funny and serious, of ugly and beautiful—are essentially *middle-class* notions; my taste in books and food and clothes, my sense of honour, my table manners, my turns of speech, my accent, even the characteristic movements of my body, are the products of a special kind of upbringing and a special niche about half-way up the social hierarchy. When I grasp this I grasp that it is no use clapping a proletarian on the back and telling him that he is as good a man as I am; if I want real contact with him, I have got to make an effort for which very likely I am unprepared. For to get outside the class-racket I have got to suppress not merely my private snobbishness, but most of my other tastes and prejudices as well. I have got to alter myself so completely that at the end I should hardly be recognisable as the same person. What is involved is not merely the amelioration of working-class conditions, nor an avoidance of the more stupid forms of snobbery, but a complete abandonment of the upper-class and middle-class attitude to life. And whether I say Yes or No probably depends upon the extent to which I grasp what is demanded of me.

Many people, however, imagine that they can abolish class-distinctions without making any uncomfortable change in their own habits and " ideology." Hence the eager class-breaking activities which one can see in progress on all sides. Everywhere there are people of good will who quite honestly believe that they are working for the overthrow of class-distinctions. The middle-class Socialist enthuses over the proletariat and runs " summer schools " where the proletarian and the repentant bourgeois are supposed to fall upon one another's necks and be brothers for ever; and the bourgeois visitors come away saying how wonderful and inspiring it has all been (the proletarian ones come away saying something different). And then there is the outer-suburban creeping Jesus, a hangover from the William Morris period, but still surprisingly common, who goes about saying " Why must we level *down*? Why not level *up*? " and proposes to level the working class " up " (up to his own standard) by means of hygiene, fruit-juice, birth-control, poetry, etc. Even the Duke of York (now King George VI) runs a yearly camp where public-school boys and boys from the slums are supposed to mix on exactly equal terms, and *do* mix for the time being, rather like the animals in one of those " Happy Family " cages where a dog, a cat, two ferrets, a rabbit and three canaries preserve an armed truce while the showman's eye is on them.

All such deliberate, conscious efforts at class-breaking are, I am convinced, a very serious mistake. Sometimes they are merely futile, but where they do show a definite result it is usually to *intensify* class-prejudice. This, if you come to think of it, is only what might be expected. You have forced the pace and set up an uneasy, unnatural equality between class and class; the resultant friction brings to the surface all kinds of feelings that might otherwise have remained buried, perhaps for ever. As I said apropos of Galsworthy, the opinions of the sentimentalist change into their opposites at the first touch of reality. Scratch the average pacifist and you find a jingo. The middle-class I.L.P.'er and the bearded fruit-juice drinker are all for a classless society so long as they see the proletariat through the wrong end of the telescope; force them into any *real* contact with a proletarian—let them get into a fight with a drunken fish-porter on Saturday night, for instance—and they are capable of swinging back to the most ordinary middle-class snobbishness. Most middle-class Socialists, however, are very unlikely to get into fights with drunken fish-porters; when they do make a genuine contact with the working class, it is usually with the working-class intelligentsia. But the working-class intelligentsia is sharply divisible into two different types. There is the type who remains working-class—who goes on working as a mechanic or a dock-labourer or whatever it may be and does not bother to change his working-class accent and habits, but who " improves his mind " in his spare time and works for the I.L.P. or the Communist Party; and there is the type who does alter his way of life, at least externally, and who by means of State scholarships succeeds in climbing into the middle class. The first is one of the finest types of man we have. I can think of some I have met whom not even the most hidebound Tory could help liking and admiring. The other type, with exceptions—D. H. Lawrence, for example—is less admirable.

To begin with, it is a pity, though it is a natural result

of the scholarship system, that the proletariat should tend to interpenetrate the middle class via the literary intelligentsia. For it is not easy to crash your way into the literary intelligentsia if you happen to be a decent human being. The modern English literary world, at any rate the highbrow section of it, is a sort of poisonous jungle where only weeds can flourish. It is just possible to be a literary gent and to keep your decency if you are a definitely *popular* writer—a writer of detective stories, for instance; but to be a highbrow, with a footing in the snootier magazines, means delivering yourself over to horrible campaigns of wire-pulling and backstairs-crawling. In the highbrow world you " get on," if you " get on " at all, not so much by your literary ability as by being the life and soul of cocktail parties and kissing the bums of verminous little lions. This, then, is the world that most readily opens its doors to the proletarian who is climbing out of his own class. The " clever " boy of a working-class family, the sort of boy who wins scholar-ships and is obviously not fitted for a life of manual labour, may find other ways of rising into the class above—a slightly different type, for instance, rises via Labour Party politics—but the literary way is by far the most usual. Literary London now teems with young men who are of proletarian origin and have been educated by means of scholarships. Many of them are very disagree-able people, quite unrepresentative of their class, and it is most unfortunate that when a person of bourgeois origin does succeed in meeting a proletarian face to face on equal terms, this is the type he most commonly meets. For the result is to drive the bourgeois, who has idealised the proletariat so long as he knew nothing about them, back into frenzies of snobbishness. The process is some-times very comic to watch, if you happen to be watching it from the outside. The poor well-meaning bourgeois, eager to embrace his proletarian brother, leaps forward with open arms; and only a little while later he is in retreat, minus a borrowed five pounds and exclaiming dolefully, " But, dash it, the fellow's not a gentleman ! "

The thing that disconcerts the bourgeois in a contact of this kind is to find certain of his own professions being taken seriously. I have pointed out that the left-wing opinions of the average " intellectual " are mainly spurious. From pure imitativeness he jeers at things which in fact he believes in. As one example out of many, take the public-school code of honour, with its " team spirit " and " Don't hit a man when he's down," and all the rest of that familiar bunkum. Who has not laughed at it ? Who, calling himself an " intellectual," would dare *not* to laugh at it ? But it is a bit different when you meet somebody who laughs at it *from the outside*; just as we spend our lives in abusing England but grow very angry when we hear a foreigner saying exactly the same things. No one has been more amusing about the public schools than " Beachcomber " of the *Express*. He laughs, quite rightly, at the ridiculous code which makes cheating at cards the worst of all sins. But would " Beachcomber " like it if one of his own friends was caught cheating at cards ? I doubt it. It is only when you meet someone of a different culture from yourself that you begin to realise what your own beliefs really are. If you are a bourgeois " intellectual " you too readily imagine that you have somehow become un-bourgeois because you find it easy to laugh at patriotism and the C. of E. and the Old School Tie and Colonel Blimp and all the rest of it. But from the point of view of the proletarian " intellectual," who at least by origin is genuinely outside the bourgeois culture, your resemblances to Colonel Blimp may be more important than your differences. Very likely he looks upon you and Colonel Blimp as practically equivalent persons; and in a way he is right, though neither you nor Colonel Blimp would admit it. So that the meeting of proletarian and bourgeois, when they do succeed in meeting, is not always the embrace of long-lost brothers; too often it is the clash of alien cultures which can only meet in war.

I have been looking at this from the point of view of the bourgeois who finds his secret beliefs challenged and is driven back to a frightened conservatism. But one has also got to consider the antagonism that is aroused in the proletarian " intellectual." By his own efforts and sometimes with frightful agonies he has struggled out of his own class into another where he expects to find a wider freedom and a greater intellectual refinement; and all he finds, very often, is a sort of hollowness, a deadness, a lack of any warm human feeling—of any real life whatever. Sometimes the bourgeoisie seem to him just dummies with money and water in their veins instead of blood. This at any rate is what he *says*, and almost any young highbrow of proletarian origin will spin you this line of talk. Hence the " proletarian " cant from which we now suffer. Everyone knows, or ought to know by this time, how it runs: the bourgeoisie are " dead " (a favourite word of abuse nowadays and very effective because meaningless), bourgeois culture is bankrupt, bourgeois " values " are despicable, and so on and so forth; if you want examples, see any number of the *Left Review* or any of the younger Communist writers such as Alec Brown, Philip Henderson, etc. The sincerity of much of this is suspect, but D. H. Lawrence, who was sincere, whatever else he may not have been, expresses the same thought over and over again. It is curious how he harps upon that idea that the English bourgeoisie are all *dead*, or at least gelded. Mellors, the gamekeeper in *Lady Chatterley's Lover* (really Lawrence himself) has had the opportunity to get out of his own class and does not particularly want to return to it, because English working people have various " disagreeable habits "; on the other hand the bourgeoisie, with whom he has also mixed to some extent, seem to him half dead, a race of eunuchs. Lady Chatterley's husband, symbolically, is impotent in the actual physical sense. And then there is the poem about the young man (once again Lawrence himself) who " got up to the top of the tree " but came down saying:

> " *Oh you've got to be like a monkey*
> *if you climb up the tree !*
> *You've no more use for the solid earth*
> *and the lad you used to be.*
> *You sit in the boughs and gibber*
> *with superiority.*
>
> *They all gibber and gibber and chatter,*
> *and never a word they say*
> *comes really out of their guts, lad,*
> *they make it up half way. . . .*
>
> *I tell you something's been done to 'em,*
> *to the pullets up above;*
> *there's not a cock bird among 'em,*" etc., etc.

You could hardly have it in plainer terms than that. Possibly by the people at " the top of the tree " Lawrence only means the real bourgeoisie, those in the £2,000 a year class and over, but I doubt it. More probably he means everyone who is more or less within the bourgeois culture—everyone who was brought up with a mincing accent and in a house where there were one or two

servants. And at this point you realise the danger of
the " proletarian " cant—realise, I mean, the terrible
antagonism that it is capable of arousing. For when
you come to such an accusation as this, you are up
against a blank wall. Lawrence tells me that because I
have been to a public school I am a eunuch. Well,
what about it? I can produce medical evidence to the
contrary, but what good will that do? Lawrence's
condemnation remains. If you tell me I am a scoundrel
I may mend my ways, but if you tell me I am a eunuch
you are tempting me to hit back in any way that seems
feasible. If you want to make an enemy of a man, tell
him that his ills are incurable.

This then is the net result of most meetings between
proletarian and bourgeois: they lay bare a real
antagonism which is intensified by the " proletarian "
cant, itself the product of forced contacts between class
and class. The only sensible procedure is to go slow and
not force the pace. If you secretly think of yourself as
a gentleman and as such the superior of the greengrocer's errand boy, it is far better to say so than to tell
lies about it. Ultimately you have got to drop your
snobbishness, but it is fatal to pretend to drop it before
you are really ready to do so.

Meanwhile one can observe on every side that dreary
phenomenon, the middle-class person who is an ardent
Socialist at twenty-five and a sniffish Conservative at
thirty-five. In a way his recoil is natural enough—at
any rate, one can see how his thoughts run. Perhaps a
classless society *doesn't* mean a beatific state of affairs in
which we shall all go on behaving exactly as before
except that there will be no class-hatred and no snobbishness; perhaps it means a bleak world in which all our
ideals, our codes, our tastes—our " ideology," in fact

will have no meaning. Perhaps this class-breaking business isn't so simple as it looked ! On the contrary, it is a wild ride into the darkness, and it may be that at the end of it the smile will be on the face of the tiger. With loving though slightly patronising smiles we set out to greet our proletarian brothers, and behold ! our proletarian brothers—in so far as we understand them— are not asking for our greetings, they are asking us to commit suicide. When the bourgeois sees it in *that* form he takes to flight, and if his flight is rapid enough it may carry him to Fascism.

CHAPTER XI

MEANWHILE, what about Socialism?

It hardly needs pointing out that at this moment we are in a very serious mess, so serious that even the dullest-witted people find it difficult to remain unaware of it. We are living in a world in which nobody is free, in which hardly anybody is secure, in which it is almost impossible to be honest and to remain alive. For enormous blocks of the working class the conditions of life are such as I have described in the opening chapters of this book, and there is no chance of those conditions showing any fundamental improvement. The very best the English working class can hope for is an occasional temporary decrease in unemployment when this or that industry is artificially stimulated by, for instance, rearmament. Even the middle classes, for the first time in their history, are feeling the pinch. They have not known actual hunger yet, but more and more of them find themselves floundering in a sort of deadly net of frustration in which it is harder and harder to persuade yourself that you are either happy, active or useful. Even the lucky ones at the top, the real bourgeoisie, are haunted periodically by a consciousness of the miseries below, and still more by fears of the menacing future. And this is merely a preliminary stage, in a country still rich with the loot of a hundred years. Presently there may be coming God knows what horrors —horrors of which, in this sheltered island, we have not even a traditional knowledge.

And all the while everyone who uses his brain knows that Socialism, as a world-system and wholeheartedly applied, is a way out. It would at least ensure our getting enough to eat even if it deprived us of everything else. Indeed, from one point of view, Socialism is such elementary common sense that I am sometimes amazed that it has not established itself already. The world is a raft sailing through space with, potentially, plenty of provisions for everybody; the idea that we must all co-operate and see to it that everyone does his fair share of the work and gets his fair share of the provisions, seems so blatantly obvious that one would say that no one could possibly fail to accept it unless he had some corrupt motive for clinging to the present system. Yet the fact that we have got to face is that Socialism is *not* establishing itself. Instead of going forward, the cause of Socialism is visibly going back. At this moment Socialists almost everywhere are in retreat before the onslaught of Fascism, and events are moving at terrible speed. As I write this the Spanish Fascist forces are bombarding Madrid, and it is quite likely that before the book is printed we shall have another Fascist country to add to the list, not to mention a Fascist control of the Mediterranean which may have the effect of delivering British foreign policy into the hands of Mussolini. I do not, however, want here to discuss the wider political issues. What I am concerned with is the fact that Socialism is losing ground exactly where it ought to be gaining it. With so much in its favour—for every empty belly is an argument for Socialism—the *idea* of Socialism is less widely accepted than it was ten years ago. The average thinking person nowadays is not merely not a Socialist, he is actively hostile to Socialism. This must be due chiefly to mistaken methods of propaganda. It means that Socialism, in the form in which it is now presented to us, has about it something inherently distasteful—something that drives away the very people who ought to be flocking to its support.

A few years ago this might have seemed unimportant. It seems only yesterday that Socialists, especially orthodox Marxists, were telling me with superior smiles that Socialism was going to arrive of its own accord by some mysterious process called "historic necessity." Possibly that belief still lingers, but it has been shaken, to say the least of it. Hence the sudden attempts of Communists in various countries to ally themselves with democratic forces which they have been sabotaging for years past. At a moment like this it is desperately necessary to discover just *why* Socialism has failed in its appeal. And it is no use writing off the current distaste for Socialism as the product of stupidity or corrupt motives. If you want to remove that distaste you have got to understand it, which means getting inside the mind of the ordinary objector to Socialism, or at least regarding his viewpoint sympathetically. No case is really answered until it has had a fair hearing. Therefore, rather paradoxically, in order to defend Socialism it is necessary to start by attacking it.

In the last three chapters I tried to analyse the difficulties that are raised by our anachronistic class-system; I shall have to touch on that subject again, because I believe that the present intensely stupid handling of the class-issue may stampede quantities of potential Socialists into Fascism. In the chapter following this one I want to discuss certain underlying assumptions that alienate sensitive minds from Socialism. But in the present chapter I am merely dealing with the obvious, preliminary objections—the kind of thing that

the person who is not a Socialist (I don't mean the
" Where's the money to come from? " type) always
starts by saying when you tax him on the subject. Some
of these objections may appear frivolous or self-con-
tradictory, but that is beside the point; I am merely
discussing symptoms. Anything is relevant which helps
to make clear why Socialism is not accepted. And please
notice that I am arguing *for* Socialism, not *against* it.
But for the moment I am *advocatus diaboli*. I am making
out a case for the sort of person who is in sympathy
with the fundamental aims of Socialism, who has the
brains to see that Socialism would " work," but who
in practice always takes to flight when Socialism is
mentioned.

Question a person of this type, and you will often get
the semi-frivolous answer: " I don't object to Socialism,
but I do object to Socialists." Logically it is a poor
argument, but it carries weight with many people. As
with the Christian religion, the worst advertisement
for Socialism is its adherents.

The first thing that must strike any outside observer is
that Socialism in its developed form is a theory confined
entirely to the middle class. The typical Socialist is not,
as tremulous old ladies imagine, a ferocious-looking
working man with greasy overalls and a raucous voice.
He is either a youthful snob-Bolshevik who in five years'
time will quite probably have made a wealthy marriage
and been converted to Roman Catholicism; or, still
more typically, a prim little man with a white-collar job,
usually a secret teetotaller and often with vegetarian
leanings, with a history of Nonconformity behind him,
and, above all, with a social position which he has no
intention of forfeiting. This last type is surprisingly
common in Socialist parties of every shade; it has perhaps

been taken over *en bloc* from the old Liberal Party. In addition to this there is the horrible—the really disquieting—prevalence of cranks wherever Socialists are gathered together. One sometimes gets the impression that the mere words " Socialism " and " Communism " draw towards them with magnetic force every fruit-juice drinker, nudist, sandal-wearer, sex-maniac, Quaker, " Nature Cure " quack, pacifist and feminist in England. One day this summer I was riding through Letchworth when the bus stopped and two dreadful-looking old men got on to it. They were both about sixty, both very short, pink and chubby, and both hatless. One of them was obscenely bald, the other had long grey hair bobbed in the Lloyd George style. They were dressed in pistachio-coloured shirts and khaki shorts into which their huge bottoms were crammed so tightly that you could study every dimple. Their appearance created a mild stir of horror on top of the bus. The man next to me, a commercial traveller I should say, glanced at me, at them, and back again at me, and murmured, " Socialists," as who should say, " Red Indians." He was probably right—the I.L.P. were holding their summer school at Letchworth. But the point is that to him, as an ordinary man, a crank meant a Socialist and a Socialist meant a crank. Any Socialist, he probably felt, could be counted on to have *something* eccentric about him. And some such notion seems to exist even among Socialists themselves. For instance, I have here a prospectus from another summer school which states its terms per week and then asks me to say " whether my diet is ordinary or vegetarian." They take it for granted, you see, that it is necessary to ask this question. This kind of thing is by itself sufficient to alienate plenty of decent people. And their instinct is perfectly sound, for the food-crank is by definition a person willing to cut himself off from human society in hopes of adding five years on to the life of his carcase; that is, a person out of touch with common humanity.

To this you have got to add the ugly fact that most middle-class Socialists, while theoretically pining for a classless society, cling like glue to their miserable fragments of social prestige. I remember my sensations of horror on first attending an I.L.P. branch meeting in London. (It might have been rather different in the North, where the bourgeoisie are less thickly scattered.) Are *these* mingy little beasts, I thought, the champions of the working class? For every person there, male and female, bore the worst stigmata of sniffish middle-class superiority. If a real working man, a miner dirty from the pit, for instance, had suddenly walked into their midst, they would have been embarrassed, angry, and disgusted; some, I should think, would have fled holding their noses. You can see the same tendency in Socialist literature, which, even when it is not openly written *de haut en bas*, is always completely removed from the working class in idiom and manner of thought. The Coles, Webbs, Stracheys, etc., are not *exactly* proletarian writers. It is doubtful whether anything describable as proletarian literature now exists—even the *Daily Worker* is written in standard South English—but a good music-hall comedian comes nearer to producing it than any Socialist writer I can think of. As for the technical jargon of the Communists, it is as far removed from the common speech as the language of a mathematical text-book. I remember hearing a professional Communist speaker address a working-class audience. His speech was the usual bookish stuff, full of long sentences and parentheses and " Notwithstanding " and " Be that as it may," besides the usual jargon of "ideology" and "class-consciousness" and "proletarian solidarity" and all the rest of it. After him a Lancashire working man got up and spoke to the crowd in their own broad lingo. There was not much doubt which of the two was nearer to his audience, but I do not suppose for a moment that the Lancashire working man was an orthodox Communist.

For it must be remembered that a working man, so long as he remains a genuine working man, is seldom or never a Socialist in the complete, logically consistent sense. Very likely he votes Labour, or even Communist if he gets the chance, but his conception of Socialism is quite different from that of the book-trained Socialist higher up. To the ordinary working man, the sort you would meet in any pub on Saturday night, Socialism does not mean much more than better wages and shorter hours and nobody bossing you about. To the more revolutionary type, the type who is a hunger-marcher and is blacklisted by employers, the word is a sort of rallying-cry against the forces of oppression, a vague threat of future violence. But, so far as my experience goes, no genuine working man grasps the deeper implications of Socialism. Often, in my opinion, he is a truer Socialist than the orthodox Marxist, because he does remember, what the other so often forgets, that Socialism means justice and common decency. But what he does not grasp is that Socialism cannot be narrowed down to mere economic justice and that a reform of that magnitude is bound to work immense changes in our civilisation and his own way of life. His vision of the Socialist future is a vision of present society with the worst abuses left out, and with interest centring round the same things as at present—family life, the pub, football, and local politics. As for the philosophic side of Marxism, the pea-and-thimble trick with those three mysterious entities, thesis, antithesis, and synthesis, I have never met a working man who had the faintest interest in it. It is of course true that plenty of people of working-class *origin* are Socialists of the theoretical bookish type. But they are never people who have *remained* working men; they don't work with their hands, that is. They belong either to the type I mentioned in the last chapter, the type who squirms into the middle class via the literary intelligentsia, or the type who becomes a Labour M.P. or a high-up trade-union official. This last type is one of the most desolating spectacles the world contains. He has been picked out to fight for his mates, and all it means to him is a soft job and the chance of " bettering " himself. Not merely while but *by* fighting the bourgeoisie he becomes a bourgeois himself. And meanwhile it is quite possible that he has remained an orthodox Marxist. But I have yet to meet a *working* miner, steel-worker, cotton-weaver, docker, navvy or whatnot who was " ideologically " sound.

One of the analogies between Communism and Roman Catholicism is that only the " educated " are completely orthodox. The most immediately striking thing about the English Roman Catholics—I don't mean the real Catholics, I mean the converts: Ronald Knox, Arnold Lunn *et hoc genus*—is their intense self-consciousness. Apparently they never think, certainly they never write, about anything but the fact that they *are* Roman Catholics; this single fact and the self-praise resulting from it form the entire stock-in-trade of the Catholic literary man. But the really interesting thing about these people is the way in which they have worked out the supposed implications of orthodoxy until the

tiniest details of life are involved. Even the liquids you
drink, apparently, can be orthodox or heretical; hence
the campaigns of Chesterton, " Beachcomber," etc.,
against tea and in favour of beer. According to Chesterton, tea-drinking is " pagan," while beer-drinking is
" Christian," and coffee is " the puritan's opium." It is
unfortunate for this theory that Catholics abound in the
" Temperance " movement and the greatest tea-boozers
in the world are the Catholic Irish; but what I am
interested in here is the attitude of mind that can make
even food and drink an occasion for religious intolerance.
A working-class Catholic would never be so absurdly
consistent as that. He does not spend his time in brooding
on the fact that he is a Roman Catholic, and he is not
particularly conscious of being different from his non-
Catholic neighbours. Tell an Irish dock-labourer in the
slums of Liverpool that his cup of tea is " pagan," and he
will call you a fool. And even in more serious matters
he does not always grasp the implications of his faith. In
the Roman Catholic homes of Lancashire you see the
crucifix on the wall and the *Daily Worker* on the table.
It is only the " educated " man, especially the literary
man, who knows how to be a bigot. And, *mutatis mutandis*,
it is the same with Communism. The creed is never
found in its pure form in a genuine proletarian.

It may be said, however, that even if the theoretical
book-trained Socialist is not a working man himself, at
least he is actuated by a love of the working class. He is
endeavouring to shed his bourgeois status and fight on
the side of the proletariat—that, obviously, must be his
motive.

But is it ? Sometimes I look at a Socialist—the intellectual, tract-writing type of Socialist, with his pullover,
his fuzzy hair, and his Marxian quotation—and wonder

what the devil his motive really *is*. It is often difficult to believe that it is a love of anybody, especially of the working class, from whom he is of all people the furthest removed. The underlying motive of many Socialists, I believe, is simply a hypertrophied sense of order. The present state of affairs offends them not because it causes misery, still less because it makes freedom impossible, but because it is untidy; what they desire, basically, is to reduce the world to something resembling a chess-board. Take the plays of a lifelong Socialist like Shaw. How much understanding or even awareness of working-class life do they display? Shaw himself declares that you can only bring a working man on the stage " as an object of compassion "; in practice he doesn't bring him on even as that, but merely as a sort of W. W. Jacobs figure of fun—the ready-made comic East Ender, like those in *Major Barbara* and *Captain Brassbound's Conversion.* At best his attitude to the working class is the sniggering *Punch* attitude, in more serious moments (consider, for instance, the young man who symbolises the dispossessed classes in *Misalliance*) he finds them merely contemptible and disgusting. Poverty and, what is more, the habits of mind created by poverty, are something to be abolished *from above*, by violence if necessary; perhaps even preferably by violence. Hence his worship of " great " men and appetite for dictatorships, Fascist or Communist; for to him, apparently (*vide* his remarks apropos of the Italo-Abyssinian war and the Stalin-Wells conversations), Stalin and Mussolini are almost equivalent persons. You get the same thing in a more mealy-mouthed form in Mrs. Sidney Webb's auto-biography, which gives, unconsciously, a most revealing picture of the high-minded Socialist slum-visitor. The truth is that to many people, calling themselves Socialists, revolution does not mean a movement of the masses with which they hope to associate themselves; it means a set of reforms which " we," the clever ones, are going to impose upon " them," the Lower Orders. On the other hand, it would be a mistake to regard the book-trained Socialist as a bloodless creature entirely incapable of emotion. Though seldom giving much evidence of affection for the exploited, he is perfectly capable of displaying hatred—a sort of queer, theoretical, *in vacuo* hatred—against the exploiters. Hence the grand old Socialist sport of denouncing the bourgeoisie. It is strange how easily almost any Socialist writer can lash himself into frenzies of rage against the class to which, by birth or by adoption, he himself invariably belongs. Sometimes the hatred of bourgeois habits and " ideology " is so far-reaching that it extends even to bourgeois characters in books. According to Henri Barbusse, the characters in the novels of Proust, Gide, etc., are " characters whom one would dearly love to have at the other side of a barricade." " A barricade," you observe. Judging from *Le Feu*, I should have thought Barbusse's experience of barricades had left him with a distaste for them. But the imaginary bayoneting of " bourgeois," who presumably don't hit back, is a bit different from the real article.

The best example of bourgeois-baiting literature that I have yet come across is Mirsky's *Intelligentsia of Great Britain*. This is a very interesting and ably-written book, and it should be read by everyone who wants to understand the rise of Fascism. Mirsky (formerly Prince Mirsky) was a White Russian *émigré* who came to England and was for some years a lecturer in Russian literature at London University. Later he was converted to Communism, returned to Russia, and produced this book as a sort of

" show-up " of the British intelligentsia from a Marxist standpoint. It is a viciously malignant book, with an unmistakable note of " Now I'm out of your reach I can say what I like about you " running all through it, and apart from a general distortion it contains some quite definite and probably intentional misrepresentation: as, for instance, when Conrad is declared to be " no less imperialist than Kipling," and D. H. Lawrence is described as writing " bare-bodied pornography " and as having " succeeded in erasing all clues to his proletarian origin "—as though Lawrence had been a porkbutcher climbing into the House of Lords ! This kind of thing is very disquieting when one remembers that it is addressed to a Russian audience who have no means of checking its accuracy. But what I am thinking of at the moment is the effect of such a book on the English public. Here you have a literary man of aristocratic extraction, a man who had probably never in his life spoken to a working man on anything approaching equal terms, uttering venomous screams of libel against his " bourgeois " colleagues. Why ? So far as appearances go, from pure malignity. He is battling *against* the British intelligentsia, but what is he battling *for* ? Within the book itself there is no indication. Hence the net effect of books like this is to give outsiders the impression that there is nothing in Communism except *hatred*. And here once again you come upon that queer resemblance between Communism and (convert) Roman Catholicism. If you want to find a book as evil-spirited as *The Intelligentsia of Great Britain*, the likeliest place to look is among the popular Roman Catholic apologists. You will find there the same venom and the same dishonesty, though, to do the Catholic justice, you will not usually find the same bad manners. Queer that Comrade

Mirsky's spiritual brother should be Father —— —— !
The Communist and the Catholic are not saying the
same thing, in a sense they are even saying opposite
things, and each would gladly boil the other in oil if
circumstances permitted; but from the point of view of
an outsider they are very much alike.

The fact is that Socialism, *in the form in which it is now
presented*, appeals chiefly to unsatisfactory or even inhuman types. On the one hand you have the warm-
hearted unthinking Socialist, the typical working-class
Socialist, who only wants to abolish poverty and does
not always grasp what this implies. On the other hand,
you have the intellectual, book-trained Socialist, who
understands that it is necessary to throw our present
civilisation down the sink and is quite willing to do so.
And this type is drawn, to begin with, entirely from the
middle class, and from a rootless town-bred section of
the middle class at that. Still more unfortunately, it
includes—so much so that to an outsider it even appears
to be composed of—the kind of people I have been
discussing; the foaming denouncers of the bourgeoisie,
and the more-water-in-your-beer reformers of whom
Shaw is the prototype, and the astute young social-
literary climbers who are Communists now, as they will
be Fascists five years hence, because it is all the go, and
all that dreary tribe of high-minded women and sandal-
wearers and bearded fruit-juice drinkers who come
flocking towards the smell of " progress " like blue-
bottles to a dead cat. The ordinary decent person, who
is in sympathy with the *essential* aims of Socialism, is
given the impression that there is no room for his kind
in any Socialist party that means business. Worse, he is
driven to the cynical conclusion that Socialism is a kind
of doom which is probably coming but must be staved

off as long as possible. Of course, as I have suggested already, it is not strictly fair to judge a movement by its adherents; but the point is that people invariably do so, and that the popular conception of Socialism is coloured by the conception of a Socialist as a dull or disagreeable person. " Socialism " is pictured as a state of affairs in which our more vocal Socialists would feel thoroughly at home. This does great harm to the cause. The ordinary man may not flinch from a dictatorship of the proletariat, if you offer it tactfully; offer him a dictatorship of the prigs, and he gets ready to fight.

There is a widespread feeling that any civilisation in which Socialism was a reality would bear the same relation to our own as a brand-new bottle of colonial burgundy bears to a few spoonfuls of first-class Beaujolais. We live, admittedly, amid the wreck of a civilisation, but it has been a great civilisation in its day, and in patches it still flourishes almost undisturbed. It still has its bouquet, so to speak; whereas the imagined Socialist future, like the colonial burgundy, tastes only of iron and water. Hence the fact, which is really a disastrous one, that artists of any consequence can never be persuaded into the Socialist fold. This is particularly the case with the writer whose political opinions are more directly and obviously connected with his work than those of, say, a painter. If one faces facts one must admit that nearly everything describable as Socialist literature is dull, tasteless, and bad. Consider the situation in England at the present moment. A whole generation has grown up more or less in familiarity with the idea of Socialism; and yet the high-water mark, so to speak, of Socialist literature is W. H. Auden, a sort of gutless Kipling, and the even feebler poets who are associated with him. Every writer of consequence and

every book worth reading is on the other side. I am
willing to believe that it is otherwise in Russia—about
which I know nothing, however—for presumably in
post-revolutionary Russia the mere violence of events
would tend to throw up a vigorous literature of sorts.
But it is certain that in Western Europe Socialism has
produced no literature worth having. A little while ago,
when the issues were less clear, there were writers of
some vitality who called themselves Socialists, but they
were using the word as a vague label. Thus, if Ibsen
and Zola described themselves as Socialists it did not
mean much more than that they were " progressives,"
while in the case of Anatole France it meant merely
that he was an anticlerical. The real Socialist writers,
the propagandist writers, have always been dull, empty
windbags—Shaw, Barbusse, Upton Sinclair, William
Morris, Waldo Frank, etc., etc. I am not, of course,
suggesting that Socialism is to be condemned because
literary gents don't like it; I am not even suggesting
that it ought necessarily to produce literature on its own
account, though I do think it a bad sign that it has
produced no songs worth singing. I am merely pointing
to the fact that writers of genuine talent are usually
indifferent to Socialism, and sometimes actively and
mischievously hostile. And this is a disaster, not only for
the writers themselves, but for the cause of Socialism,
which has great need of them.

   This, then, is the superficial aspect of the ordinary
man's recoil from Socialism. I know the whole dreary
argument very thoroughly, because I know it from both
sides. Everything that I say here I have both said to
ardent Socialists who were trying to convert me, and
had said to me by bored non-Socialists whom I was
trying to convert. The whole thing amounts to a kind

of *malaise* produced by dislike of individual Socialists, especially of the cocksure Marx-quoting type. Is it childish to be influenced by that kind of thing? Is it silly? Is it even contemptible? It is all that, but the point is that *it happens*, and therefore it is important to keep it in mind.

CHAPTER XII

HOWEVER, there is a much more serious difficulty than the local and temporary objections which I discussed in the last chapter.

Faced by the fact that intelligent people are so often on the other side, the Socialist is apt to set it down to corrupt motives (conscious or unconscious), or to an ignorant belief that Socialism would not "work," or to a mere dread of the horrors and discomforts of the revolutionary period before Socialism is established. Undoubtedly all these are important, but there are plenty of people who are influenced by none of them and are nevertheless hostile to Socialism. Their reason for recoiling from Socialism is spiritual, or "ideological." They object to it not on the ground that it would not "work," but precisely because it would "work" too well. What they are afraid of is not the things that are going to happen in their own lifetime, but the things that are going to happen in the remote future when Socialism is a reality.

I have very seldom met a convinced Socialist who could grasp that thinking people may be repelled by the *objective* towards which Socialism appears to be moving. The Marxist, especially, dismisses this kind of thing as bourgeois sentimentality. Marxists as a rule are not very good at reading the minds of their adversaries; if they were, the situation in Europe might be less desperate than it is at present. Possessing a technique which seems to explain everything, they do not often bother to discover what is going on inside other people's heads. Here, for instance, is an illustration of the kind of thing I mean. Discussing the widely held theory—which in one sense is certainly true—that Fascism is a product of Communism, Mr. N. A. Holdaway, one of the ablest Marxist writers we possess, writes as follows:

" The hoary legend of Communism leading to Fascism. . . . The element of truth in it is this: that the appearance of Communist activity warns the ruling class that democratic Labour Parties are no longer capable of holding the working class in check, and that capitalist dictatorship must assume another form if it is to survive."

You see here the defects of the method. Because he has detected the underlying economic cause of Fascism, he tacitly assumes that the spiritual side of it is of no importance. Fascism is written off as a manœuvre of the " ruling class," which at bottom it is. But this in itself would only explain why Fascism appeals to capitalists. What about the millions who are not capitalists, who in a material sense have nothing to gain from Fascism and are often aware of it, and who, nevertheless, are Fascists? Obviously their approach has been purely along the ideological line. They could only be stampeded into Fascism because Communism attacked or seemed to attack certain things (patriotism, religion, etc.) which lay deeper than the economic motive; and in *that* sense it is perfectly true that Communism leads to Fascism. It is a pity that Marxists nearly always concentrate on letting economic cats out of ideological bags; it does in one sense reveal the truth, but with this penalty, that most of their propaganda misses its mark. It is the spiritual recoil from Socialism, especially as it manifests itself in sensitive people, that I want to discuss in this chapter. I shall have to analyse it at some length, because it is very widespread, very powerful and, among Socialists, almost completely ignored.

The first thing to notice is that the idea of Socialism is bound up, more or less inextricably, with the idea of machine-production. Socialism is essentially an *urban* creed. It grew up more or less concurrently with industrialism, it has always had its roots in the town proletariat and the town intellectual, and it is doubtful whether it could ever have arisen in any but an industrial society. Granted industrialism, the idea of Socialism presents itself naturally, because private ownership is only tolerable when every individual (or family or other unit) is at least moderately self-supporting; but the effect of industrialism is to make it impossible for anyone to be self-supporting even for a moment. Industrialism, once it rises above a fairly low level, *must* lead to some form of collectivism. Not necessarily to Socialism, of course; conceivably it might lead to the Slave-State of which Fascism is a kind of prophecy. And the converse is also true. Machine-production suggests Socialism, but Socialism as a world-system implies machine-production, because it demands certain things not compatible with a primitive way of life. It demands, for instance, constant intercommunication and exchange of goods between all parts of the earth; it demands some degree of centralised control; it demands an approximately equal standard of life for all human beings and probably a certain uniformity of education. We may take it, therefore, that any world in which Socialism was a reality would be at least as highly mechanised as the United States at this moment, probably much more so. In any case, no Socialist would think of denying this. The Socialist world is always pictured as a completely mechanised, immensely organised world, depending on the machine as the civilisations of antiquity depended on the slave.

So far so good, or so bad. Many, perhaps a majority, of thinking people are not in love with machine-civilisation, but everyone who is not a fool knows that it is nonsense to talk at this moment about scrapping the machine. But the unfortunate thing is that Socialism, as usually presented, is bound up with the idea of mechanical progress, not merely as a necessary development but as an end in itself, almost as a kind of religion. This idea is implicit in, for instance, most of the propagandist stuff that is written about the rapid mechanical advance in Soviet Russia (the Dneiper dam, tractors, etc., etc.). Karel Capek hits it off well enough in the horrible ending of *R.U.R.*, when the Robots, having slaughtered the last human being, announce their intention to " build many houses " (just for the sake of building houses, you see). The kind of person who most readily accepts Socialism is also the kind of person who views mechanical progress, *as such*, with enthusiasm. And this is so much the case that Socialists are often unable to grasp that the opposite opinion exists. As a rule the most persuasive argument they can think of is to tell you that the present mechanisation of the world is as nothing to what we shall see when Socialism is established. Where there is one aeroplane now, in those days there will be fifty ! All the work that is now done by hand will then be done by machinery; everything that is now made of leather, wood or stone will be made of rubber, glass or steel; there will be no disorder, no loose ends, no wildernesses, no wild animals, no weeds, no disease, no poverty, no pain—and so on and so forth. The Socialist world is to be above all things an *ordered* world, an *efficient* world. But it is precisely from that vision of the future as a sort of glittering Wells-world that sensitive minds recoil. Please notice that this essentially fat-bellied version of " progress " is not an integral part of Socialist doctrine; but it has come to be thought of as one, with the result that the temperamental conservatism which is latent in all kinds of people is easily mobilised against Socialism.

Every sensitive person has moments when he is suspicious of machinery and to some extent of physical science. But it is important to sort out the various motives, which have differed greatly at different times, for hostility to science and machinery, and to disregard the jealousy of the modern literary gent who hates science because science has stolen literature's thunder. The earliest full-length attack on science and machinery that I am acquainted with is in the third part of *Gulliver's Travels*. But Swift's attack, though brilliant as a *tour de force*, is irrelevant and even silly, because it is written from the standpoint—perhaps this seems a queer thing to say of the author of *Gulliver's Travels*—of a man who lacked imagination. To Swift, science was merely a kind of futile muckraking and the machines were nonsensical contraptions that would never work. His standard was that of practical usefulness, and he lacked the vision to see that an experiment which is not demonstrably useful at the moment may yield results in the future. Elsewhere in the book he names it as the best of all achievements " to make two blades of grass grow where one grew before "; not seeing, apparently, that this is just what the machine can do. A little later the despised machines began working, physical science increased its scope, and there came the celebrated conflict between religion and science which agitated our grandfathers. That conflict is over and both sides have retreated and claimed a victory, but an anti-scientific bias still lingers in the minds of most religious believers. All through the nineteenth century protesting voices were raised against science and machinery (see Dickens's *Hard Times*, for instance), but usually for the rather shallow reason that industrialism in its first stages was cruel and ugly. Samuel Butler's attack on the machine in the well-known chapter of *Erewhon* is a different matter. But Butler himself lived in a less desperate age than our own, an age in which it was still possible for a first-rate man to be a dilettante part of the time, and therefore the whole thing appeared to him as a kind of intellectual exercise. He saw clearly enough our abject dependence on the machine, but instead of bothering to work out its consequences he preferred to exaggerate it for the sake of what was not much more than a joke. It is only in our own age, when mechanisation has finally triumphed, that we can actually *feel* the tendency of the machine to make a fully human life impossible. There is probably no one capable of thinking and feeling who has not occasionally looked at a gaspipe chair and reflected that the machine is the enemy of life. As a rule, however, this feeling is instinctive rather than reasoned. People know that in some way or another " progress " is a swindle, but they reach this conclusion by a kind of mental shorthand; my job here is to supply the logical steps that are usually left out. But first one must ask, what is the function of the machine? Obviously its primary function is to save work, and the type of person to whom machine-civilisation is entirely acceptable seldom sees any reason for looking further. Here for instance is a person who claims; or rather screams, that he is thoroughly at home in the modern mechanised world.

I am quoting from *World Without Faith*, by Mr. John Beevers. This is what he says:

" It is plain lunacy to say that the average £2 10s. to £4 a week man of to-day is a lower type than an eighteenth-century farm labourer. Or than the labourer or peasant of any exclusively agricultural community now or in the past. It just isn't true. It is so damn silly to cry out about the civilising effects of work in the fields and farmyards as against that done in a big locomotive works or an automobile factory. Work is a nuisance. We work because we have to and all work is done to provide us with leisure and the means of spending that leisure as enjoyably as possible."

And again:

" Man is going to have time enough and power enough to hunt for his own heaven on earth without worrying about the supernatural one. The earth will be so pleasant a place that the priest and the parson won't be left with much of a tale to tell. Half the stuffing is knocked out of them by one neat blow." Etc., etc., etc.

There is a whole chapter to this effect (Chapter IV of Mr. Beevers's book), and it is of some interest as an exhibition of machine-worship in its most completely vulgar, ignorant and half-baked form. It is the authentic voice of a large section of the modern world. Every aspirin-eater in the outer suburbs would echo it fervently. Notice the shrill wail of anger (" It just isn't troo-o-o ! " etc.) with which Mr. Beevers meets the suggestion that his grandfather may have been a better man than himself; and the still more horrible suggestion that if we returned to a simpler way of life he might have to toughen his muscles with a job of work. Work, you see, is done " to provide us with leisure." Leisure for what ? Leisure to become more like Mr. Beevers, presumably.

Though as a matter of fact, from that line of talk about " heaven on earth," you can make a fairly good guess at what he would like civilisation to be; a sort of Lyons Corner House lasting *in sæcula sæculorum* and getting bigger and noisier all the time. And in any book by anyone who feels at home in the machine-world—in any book by H. G. Wells, for instance—you will find passages of the same kind. How often have we not heard it, that glutinously uplifting stuff about " the machines, our new race of slaves, which will set humanity free," etc., etc., etc. To these people, apparently, the only danger of the machine is its possible use for destructive purposes; as, for instance, aeroplanes are used in war. Barring wars and unforeseen disasters, the future is envisaged as an ever more rapid march of mechanical progress; machines to save work, machines to save thought, machines to save pain, hygiene, efficiency, organisation, more hygiene, more efficiency, more organisation, more machines— until finally you land up in the by now familiar Wellsian Utopia, aptly caricatured by Huxley in *Brave New World*, the paradise of little fat men. Of course in their day-dreams of the future the little fat men are neither fat nor little; they are Men Like Gods. But why should they be? All mechanical progress is towards greater and greater efficiency; ultimately, therefore, towards a world in which *nothing goes wrong*. But in a world in which nothing went wrong, many of the qualities which Mr. Wells regards as " godlike " would be no more valuable than the animal faculty of moving the ears. The beings in *Men Like Gods* and *The Dream* are represented, for example, as brave, generous and physically strong. But in a world from which physical danger had been banished—and obviously mechanical progress tends to eliminate danger—would physical courage be likely to survive? *Could* it survive? And why should physical strength survive in a world where there was never the need for physical labour? As for such qualities as loyalty, generosity, etc., in a world where nothing went wrong, they would be not only irrelevant but probably unimaginable. The truth is that many of the qualities we admire in human beings can only function in opposition to some kind of disaster, pain or difficulty; but the tendency of mechanical progress is to eliminate disaster, pain and difficulty. In books like *The Dream* and *Men Like Gods* it is assumed that such qualities as strength, courage, generosity, etc., will be kept alive because they are comely qualities and necessary attributes of a full human being. Presumably, for instance, the inhabitants of Utopia would create artificial dangers in order to exercise their courage, and do dumb-bell exercises to harden muscles which they would never be obliged to use. And here you observe the huge contradiction which is usually present in the idea of progress. The tendency of mechanical progress is to make your environment safe and soft; and yet you are striving to keep yourself brave and hard. You are at the same moment furiously pressing forward and desperately holding back. It is as though a London stockbroker should go to his office in a suit of chain mail and insist on talking medieval Latin. So in the last analysis the champion of progress is also the champion of anachronisms.

Meanwhile I am assuming that the tendency of mechanical progress *is* to make life safe and soft. This may be disputed, because at any given moment the effect of some recent mechanical invention may appear to be the opposite. Take for instance the transition from horses to motor vehicles. At a first glance one might say, considering the enormous toll of road deaths, that the motor-car does not exactly tend to make life safer. Moreover it probably needs as much toughness to be a first-rate dirt-track rider as to be a broncho-buster or to ride in the Grand National. Nevertheless the *tendency* of all machinery is to become safer and easier to handle. The danger of accidents would disappear if we chose to tackle our road-planning problem seriously, as we shall do sooner or later; and meanwhile the motor-car has evolved to a point at which anyone who is not blind or paralytic can drive it after a few lessons. Even now it needs far less nerve and skill to drive a car ordinarily well than to ride a horse ordinarily well; in twenty years time it may need no nerve or skill at all. Therefore, one must say that, taking society as a whole, the result of the transition from horses to cars has been an increase in human softness. Presently somebody comes along with another invention, the aeroplane for instance, which does not at first sight appear to make life safer. The first men who went up in aeroplanes were superlatively brave, and even to-day it must need an exceptionally good nerve to be a pilot. But the same tendency as before is at work. The aeroplane, like the motor-car, will be made foolproof; a million engineers are working, almost unconsciously, in that direction. Finally—this is the objective, though it may never quite be reached— you will get an aeroplane whose pilot needs no more skill or courage than a baby needs in its perambulator. And all mechanical progress is and must be in this direction. A machine evolves by becoming more efficient, that is, more foolproof; hence the objective of mechanical progress is a foolproof world—which may or may not mean a world inhabited by fools. Mr. Wells would probably retort that the world can never become fool-proof, because, however high a standard of efficiency you have reached, there is always some greater difficulty ahead. For example (this is Mr. Wells's favourite idea— he has used it in goodness knows how many perorations), when you have got this planet of ours perfectly into trim, you start upon the enormous task of reaching and colonising another. But this is merely to push the objective further into the future; the objective itself remains the same. Colonise another planet, and the game of mechanical progress begins anew; for the fool-proof world you have substituted the foolproof solar system—the foolproof universe. In tying yourself to the ideal of mechanical efficiency, you tie yourself to the ideal of softness. But softness is repulsive; and thus all progress is seen to be a frantic struggle towards an objective which you hope and pray will never be reached. Now and again, but not often, you meet some-body who grasps that what is usually called progress also entails what is usually called degeneracy, and who is nevertheless in favour of progress. Hence the fact that in Mr. Shaw's Utopia a statue was erected to Falstaff, as the first man who ever made a speech in favour of cowardice.

But the trouble goes immensely deeper than this. Hitherto I have only pointed out the absurdity of aiming at mechanical progress and also at the preservation of qualities which mechanical progress makes unnecessary. The question one has got to consider is whether there is *any* human activity which would not be maimed by the dominance of the machine.

The function of the machine is to save work. In a fully mechanised world all the dull drudgery will be done by machinery, leaving us free for more interesting pursuits. So expressed, this sounds splendid. It makes one sick to see half a dozen men sweating their guts out to dig a trench for a water-pipe, when some easily devised machine would scoop the earth out in a couple of minutes. Why not let the machine do the work and the men go and do something else. But presently the question arises, what else are they to do? Supposedly they are set free from " work " in order that they may do something which is not " work." But what is work and what is not work? Is it work to dig, to carpenter, to plant trees, to fell trees, to ride, to fish, to hunt, to feed chickens, to play the piano, to take photographs, to build a house, to cook, to sew, to trim hats, to mend motor bicycles? All of these things are work to somebody, and all of them are play to somebody. There are in fact very few activities which cannot be classed either as work or play according as you choose to regard them. The labourer set free from digging may want to spend his leisure, or part of it, in playing the piano, while the professional pianist may be only too glad to get out and dig at the potato patch. Hence the antithesis between work, as something intolerably tedious, and not-work, as something desirable, is false. The truth is that when a human being is not eating, drinking, sleeping, making love, talking, playing games or merely lounging about— and these things will not fill up a lifetime—he needs work and usually looks for it, though he may not call it work. Above the level of a third- or fourth-grade moron, life has got to be lived largely in terms of effort. For man is not, as the vulgarer hedonists seem to suppose, a kind of walking stomach; he has also got a hand, an eye and a brain. Cease to use your hands, and you have lopped off a huge chunk of your consciousness. And now consider again those half-dozen men who were digging the trench for the water-pipe. A machine has set them free from digging, and they are going to amuse themselves with something else—carpentering, for instance. But whatever they want to do, they will find that another machine has set them free from *that*. For in a fully mechanised world there would be no more need to carpenter, to cook, to mend motor bicycles, etc., than there would be to dig. There is scarcely anything, from catching a whale to carving a cherry stone, that could not conceivably be done by machinery. The machine would even encroach upon the activities we now class as " art "; it is doing so already, via the camera and the radio. Mechanise the world as fully as it might be mechanised, and whichever way you turn there will be some machine cutting you off from the chance of working—that is, of living.

At a first glance this might not seem to matter. Why should you not get on with your " creative work " and disregard the machines that would do it for you ? But it is not so simple as it sounds. Here am I, working eight hours a day in an insurance office; in my spare time I want to do something " creative," so I choose to do a bit of carpentering—to make myself a table, for instance. Notice that from the very start there is a touch of artificiality about the whole business, for the factories can turn me out a far better table than I can make for myself. But even when I get to work on my table, it is not possible for me to feel towards it as the cabinet-maker of a hundred years ago felt towards his table, still less as Robinson Crusoe felt towards his. For before I start, most of the work has already been done for me by machinery. The tools I use demand the minimum of skill. I can get, for instance, planes which will cut out any moulding; the cabinet-maker of a hundred years ago would have had to do the work with chisel and gouge, which demanded real skill of eye and

hand. The boards I buy are ready planed and the legs
are ready turned by the lathe. I can even go to the
wood-shop and buy all the parts of the table ready-made
and only needing to be fitted together; my work being
reduced to driving in a few pegs and using a piece of
sandpaper. And if this is so at present, in the mechanised
future it will be enormously more so. With the tools and
materials available *then*, there will be no possibility of
mistake, hence no room for skill. Making a table will
be easier and duller than peeling a potato. In such
circumstances it is nonsense to talk of " creative work."
In any case the arts of the hand (which have got to be
transmitted by apprenticeship) would long since have
disappeared. Some of them have disappeared already,
under the competition of the machine. Look round any
country churchyard and see whether you can find a
decently-cut tombstone later than 1820. The art, or
rather the craft, of stonework has died out so completely
that it would take centuries to revive it.

But it may be said, why not retain the machine *and*
retain " creative work " ? Why not cultivate anachronisms as a spare-time hobby ? Many people have played
with this idea; it seems to solve with such beautiful ease
the problems set by the machine. The citizen of Utopia,
we are told, coming home from his daily two hours of
turning a handle in the tomato-canning factory, will
deliberately revert to a more primitive way of life and
solace his creative instincts with a bit of fretwork,
pottery-glazing or handloom-weaving. And why is this
picture an absurdity—as it is, of course ? Because of a
principle that is not always recognised, though always
acted upon: that so long as the machine *is there*, one is
under an obligation to use it. No one draws water from
the well when he can turn on the tap. One sees a good

illustration of this in the matter of travel. Everyone who has travelled by primitive methods in an undeveloped country, knows that the difference between that kind of travel and modern travel in trains, cars, etc., is the difference between life and death. The nomad who walks or rides, with his baggage stowed on a camel or an ox-cart, may suffer every kind of discomfort, but at least he is living while he is travelling; whereas for the passenger in an express train or a luxury liner his journey is an interregnum, a kind of temporary death. And yet so long as the railways exist, one has got to travel by train—or by car or aeroplane. Here am I, forty miles from London. When I want to go up to London why do I not pack my luggage on to a mule and set out on foot, making a two days' march of it? Because, with the Green Line buses whizzing past me every ten minutes, such a journey would be intolerably irksome. In order that one may enjoy primitive methods of travel, it is necessary that no other method should be available. No human being ever wants to do anything in a more cumbrous way than is necessary. Hence the absurdity of that picture of Utopians saving their souls with fret-work. In a world where everything could be done by machinery, everything would be done by machinery. Deliberately to revert to primitive methods, to use archaic tools, to put silly little difficulties in your own way, would be a piece of dilettantism, of pretty-pretty arty and craftiness. It would be like solemnly sitting down to eat your dinner with stone implements. Revert to handwork in a machine age, and you are back in Ye Olde Tea Shoppe or the Tudor villa with the sham beams tacked to the wall.

The tendency of mechanical progress, then, is to frustrate the human need for effort and creation. It makes unnecessary and even impossible the activities of the eye and the hand. The apostle of " progress " will sometimes declare that this does not matter, but you can usually drive him into a corner by pointing out the horrible lengths to which the process can be carried. Why, for instance, use your hands at all—why use them even for blowing your nose or sharpening a pencil? Surely you could fix some kind of steel and rubber contraption to your shoulders and let your arms wither into stumps of skin and bone? And so with every organ and every faculty. There is really no reason why a human being should do more than eat, drink, sleep, breathe and procreate; *everything* else could be done for him by machinery. Therefore the logical end of mechanical progress is to reduce the human being to something resembling a brain in a bottle. That is the goal towards which we are already ·moving, though, of course, we have no intention of getting there; just as a man who drinks a bottle of whisky a day does not actually intend to get cirrhosis of the liver. The implied objective of " progress " is—not *exactly*, perhaps, the brain in the bottle, but at any rate some frightful subhuman depth of softness and helplessness. And the unfortunate thing is that at present the word " progress " and the word " Socialism " are linked inseparably in almost everyone's mind. The kind of person who hates machinery also takes it for granted to hate Socialism; the Socialist is always in favour of mechanisation, rationalisation, modernisation—or at least thinks that he ought to be in favour of them. Quite recently, for instance, a prominent I.L.P.'er confessed to me with a sort of wistful shame—as though it were something faintly improper—that he was " fond of horses." Horses, you see, belong to the vanished agricultural past, and

all sentiment for the past carries with it a vague smell of
heresy. I do not believe that this need necessarily be so,
but undoubtedly it is so. And in itself it is quite enough
to explain the alienation of decent minds from Socialism.

A generation ago every intelligent person was in
some sense a revolutionary; nowadays it would be
nearer the mark to say that every intelligent person
is a reactionary. In this connection it is worth comparing
H. G. Wells's *The Sleeper Awakes* with Aldous Huxley's
Brave New World, written thirty years later. Each is
a pessimistic Utopia, a vision of a sort of prig's paradise
in which all the dreams of the " progressive " person
come true. Considered merely as a piece of imaginative
construction *The Sleeper Awakes* is, I think, much superior,
but it suffers from vast contradictions because of the fact
that Wells, as the arch-priest of " progress," cannot
write with any conviction *against* " progress." He draws
a picture of a glittering, strangely sinister world in
which the privileged classes live a life of shallow gutless
hedonism, and the workers, reduced to a state of utter
slavery and sub-human ignorance, toil like troglodytes
in caverns underground. As soon as one examines this
idea—it is further developed in a splendid short story
in *Stories of Space and Time*—one sees its inconsistency.
For in the immensely mechanised world that Wells is
imagining, why should the workers have to work harder
than at present ? Obviously the tendency of the machine
is to eliminate work, not to increase it. In the machine-
world the workers might be enslaved, ill-treated and even
underfed, but they certainly would not be condemned
to ceaseless manual toil; because in that case what
would be the function of the machine ? You can have
machines doing all the work or human beings doing all
the work, but you can't have both. Those armies of

underground workers, with their blue uniforms and their debased, half-human language, are only put in " to make your flesh creep." Wells wants to suggest that " progress " might take a wrong turning; but the only evil he cares to imagine is inequality—one class grabbing all the wealth and power and oppressing the others, apparently out of pure spite. Give it quite a small twist, he seems to suggest, overthrow the privileged class—change over from world-capitalism to Socialism, in fact—and all will be well. The machine-civilisation is to continue, but its products are to be shared out equally. The thought he dare not face is that the machine itself may be the enemy. So in his more characteristic Utopias (*The Dream, Men like Gods,* etc.), he returns to optimism and to a vision of humanity, " liberated " by the machine, as a race of enlightened sunbathers whose sole topic of conversation is their own superiority to their ancestors. *Brave New World* belongs to a later time and to a generation which has seen through the swindle of " progress." It contains its own contradictions (the most important of them is pointed out in Mr. John Strachey's *The Coming Struggle for Power*), but it is at least a memorable assault on the more fat-bellied type of perfectionism. Allowing for the exaggerations of caricature, it probably expresses what a majority of thinking people feel about machine-civilisation.

The sensitive person's hostility to the machine is in one sense unrealistic, because of the obvious fact that the machine has come to stay. But as an attitude of mind there is a great deal to be said for it. The machine has got to be accepted, but it is probably better to accept it rather as one accepts a drug—that is, grudgingly and suspiciously. Like a drug, the machine is useful,

dangerous and habit-forming. The oftener one sur-
renders to it the tighter its grip becomes. You have only
to look about you at this moment to realise with what
sinister speed the machine is getting us into its power.

To begin with, there is the frightful debauchery of
taste that has already been effected by a century of
mechanisation. This is almost too obvious and too
generally admitted to need pointing out. But as a single
instance, take taste in its narrowest sense—the taste for
decent food. In the highly mechanised countries, thanks
to tinned food, cold storage, synthetic flavouring
matters, etc., the palate is almost a dead organ. As you
can see by looking at any greengrocer's shop, what the
majority of English people mean by an apple is a lump
of highly-coloured cotton wool from America or
Australia; they will devour these things, apparently
with pleasure, and let the English apples rot under the
trees. It is the shiny, standardised, machine-made look
of the American apple that appeals to them; the superior
taste of the English apple is something they simply
do not notice. Or look at the factory-made, foil-wrapped
cheeses and "blended" butter in any grocer's; look
at the hideous rows of tins which usurp more and more
of the space in any food-shop, even a dairy; look at a
sixpenny Swiss roll or a twopenny ice-cream; look at the
filthy chemical by-product that people will pour down
their throats under the name of beer. Wherever you
look you will see some slick machine-made article
triumphing over the old-fashioned article that still
tastes of something other than sawdust. And what
applies to food applies also to furniture, houses, clothes,
books, amusements and everything else that makes up
our environment. There are now millions of people,
and they are increasing every year, to whom the blaring

of a radio is not only a more acceptable but a more
normal background to their thoughts than the lowing of
cattle or the song of birds. The mechanisation of the
world could never proceed very far while taste, even
the taste-buds of the tongue, remained uncorrupted,
because in that case most of the products of the machine
would be simply unwanted. In a healthy world there
would be no demand for tinned food, aspirins, gramo-
phones, gaspipe chairs, machine guns, daily newspapers,
telephones, motor-cars, etc., etc.; and on the other hand
there would be a constant demand for the things the
machine cannot produce. But meanwhile the machine
is here, and its corrupting effects are almost irresistible.
One inveighs against it, but one goes on using it. Even
a bare-arse savage, given the chance, will learn the
vices of civilisation within a few months. Mechanisation
leads to the decay of taste, the decay of taste leads to the
demand for machine-made articles and hence to more
mechanisation, and so a vicious circle is established.

But in addition to this there is a tendency for the
mechanisation of the world to proceed as it were automatically, whether we want it or not. This is due to the
fact that in modern Western man the faculty of mechanical invention has been fed and stimulated till it has
reached almost the status of an instinct. People invent
new machines and improve existing ones almost unconsciously, rather as a somnambulist will go on working
in his sleep. In the past, when it was taken for granted
that life on this planet is harsh or at any rate laborious,
it seemed the natural fate to go on using the clumsy
implements of your forefathers, and only a few eccentric
persons, centuries apart, proposed innovations; hence
throughout enormous ages such things as the ox-cart, the
plough, the sickle, etc., remained radically unchanged.

It is on record that screws have been in use since remote antiquity and yet that it was not till the middle of the nineteenth century that anyone thought of making screws with points on them; for several thousand years they remained flat-ended and holes had to be drilled for them before they could be inserted. In our own epoch such a thing would be unthinkable. For almost every modern Western man has his inventive faculty to some extent developed; the Western man invents machines as naturally as the Polynesian islander swims. Give a Western man a job of work and he immediately begins devising a machine that would do it for him; give him a machine and he thinks of ways of improving it. I understand this tendency well enough, for in an ineffectual sort of way I have that type of mind myself. I have not either the patience or the mechanical skill to devise any machine that would work, but I am perpetually seeing, as it were, the ghosts of possible machines that might save me the trouble of using my brain or muscles. A person with a more definite mechanical turn would probably construct some of them and put them into operation. But under our present economic system, whether he constructed them—or rather, whether anyone else had the benefit of them—would depend upon whether they were commercially valuable. The Socialists are right, therefore, when they claim that the rate of mechanical progress will be much more rapid once Socialism is established. Given a mechanical civilisation the process of invention and improvement will always continue, but the tendency of capitalism is to slow it down, because under capitalism any invention which does not promise fairly immediate profits is neglected; some, indeed, which threaten to reduce profits are suppressed almost as ruthlessly as the flexible glass mentioned by Petronius.[1] Establish Socialism —remove the profit principle—and the inventor will have a free hand. The mechanisation of the world, already rapid enough, would be or at any rate could be enormously accelerated.

And this prospect is a slightly sinister one, because it is obvious even now that the process of mechanisation is out of control. It is happening merely because humanity has got the habit. A chemist perfects a new method of synthesising rubber, or a mechanic devises a new pattern of gudgeon-pin. Why? Not for any clearly understood purpose, but simply from the impulse to invent and improve, which has now become instinctive. Put a pacifist to work in a bomb-factory and in two months he will be devising a new type of bomb. Hence the appearance of such diabolical things as poison gases, which are not expected even by their inventors to be beneficial to humanity. Our attitude towards such things as poison gases *ought* to be the attitude of the king of Brobdingnag towards gunpowder; but because we live in a mechanical and scientific age we are infected with the notion that, whatever else happens, " progress " must continue and knowledge must never be suppressed. Verbally, no doubt, we would agree that machinery is made for man and not man for machinery; in practice any attempt to check the development of the machine appears to us as an attack on knowledge and therefore a kind of blasphemy. And even if the whole of humanity suddenly revolted against the machine and decided to escape to a simpler way of life, the escape would still be immensely difficult. It would not do, as in Butler's *Erewhon*, to smash every machine invented

[1] For example: Some years ago someone invented a gramophone needle that would last for decades. One of the big gramophone companies bought up the patent rights, and that was the last that was ever heard of it.

after a certain date; we should also have to smash the habit of mind that would, almost involuntarily, devise fresh machines as soon as the old ones were smashed. And in all of us there is at least a tinge of that habit of mind. In every country in the world the large army of scientists and technicians, with the rest of us panting at their heels, are marching along the road of "progress" with the blind persistence of a column of ants. Comparatively few people want it to happen, plenty of people actively want it *not* to happen, and yet it is happening. The process of mechanisation has itself become a machine, a huge glittering vehicle whirling us we are not certain where, but probably towards the padded Wells-world and the brain in the bottle.

This, then, is the case against the machine. Whether it is a sound or unsound case hardly matters. The point is that these or very similar arguments would be echoed by every person who is hostile to machine-civilisation. And unfortunately, because of that nexus of thought, "Socialism-progress-machinery-Russia-tractors-hygiene-machinery-progress," which exists in almost everyone's mind, it is usually the *same* person who is hostile to Socialism. The kind of person who hates central heating and gaspipe chairs is also the kind of person who, when you mention Socialism, murmurs something about "beehive state" and moves away with a pained expression. So far as my observation goes, very few Socialists grasp why this is so, or even that it *is* so. Get the more vocal type of Socialist into a corner, repeat to him the substance of what I have said in this chapter, and see what kind of answer you get. As a matter of fact you will get several answers; I am so familiar with them that I know them almost by heart.

In the first place he will tell you that it is impossible

to " go back " (or to " put back the hand of progress "
—as though the hand of progress hadn't been pretty
violently put back several times in human history !),
and will then accuse you of being a medievalist and
begin to descant upon the horrors of the Middle Ages,
leprosy, the Inquisition, etc. As a matter of fact, most
attacks upon the Middle Ages and the past generally
by apologists of modernity are beside the point, because
their essential trick is to project a modern man, with his
squeamishness and his high standards of comfort, into
an age when such things were unheard of. But notice
that in any case this is not an answer. For a dislike of
the mechanised future does not imply the smallest
reverence for any period of the past. D. H. Lawrence,
wiser than the medievalist, chose to idealise the Etruscans
about whom we know conveniently little. But there is
no need to idealise even the Etruscans—or the Pelasgians,
or the Aztecs, or the Sumerians, or any other vanished
and romantic people. When one pictures a desirable
civilisation, one pictures it merely as an objective;
there is no need to pretend that it has ever existed in
space and time. Press this point home, explain that you
wish merely to aim at making life simpler and harder
instead of softer and more complex, and the Socialist
will usually assume that you want to revert to a " state
of nature "—meaning some stinking palæolithic cave:
as though there were nothing between a flint scraper
and the steel mills of Sheffield, or between a skin coracle
and the *Queen Mary* !

Finally, however, you will get an answer which is
rather more to the point and which runs roughly as
follows: " Yes, what you are saying is all very well in
its way. No doubt it would be very noble to harden
ourselves and do without aspirins and central heating

and so forth. But the point is, you see, that nobody seriously wants it. It would mean going back to an agricultural way of life, which means beastly hard work and isn't at all the same thing as playing at gardening. I don't want hard work, you don't want hard work—nobody wants it who knows what it means. You only talk as you do because you've never done a day's work in your life," etc., etc.

Now this in a sense is true. It amounts to saying, " We're soft—for God's sake let's stay soft ! " which at least is realistic. As I have pointed out already, the machine has got us in its grip and to escape will be immensely difficult. Nevertheless this answer is really an evasion, because it fails to make clear what we mean when we say that we " want " this or that. I am a degenerate modern semi-intellectual who would die if I did not get my early morning cup of tea and my *New Statesman* every Friday. Clearly I do not, in a sense, " want " to return to a simpler, harder, probably agricultural way of life. In the same sense I don't " want " to cut down my drinking, to pay my debts, to take enough exercise, to be faithful to my wife, etc., etc. But in another and more permanent sense I do want these things, and perhaps in the same sense I want a civilisation in which " progress " is not definable as making the world safe for little fat men. These that I have outlined are practically the only arguments that I have been able to get from Socialists—thinking, book-trained Socialists—when I have tried to explain to them just *how* they are driving away possible adherents. Of course there is also the old argument that Socialism is going to arrive anyway, whether people like it or not, because of that trouble-saving thing, " historic necessity." But " historic necessity," or rather the belief in it, has failed to survive Hitler.

Meanwhile the thinking person, by intellect usually left-wing but by temperament often right-wing, hovers at the gate of the Socialist fold. He is no doubt aware that he *ought* to be a Socialist. But he observes first the dullness of individual Socialists, then the apparent flabbiness of Socialist ideals, and veers away. Till quite recently it was natural to veer towards indifferentism. Ten years ago, even five years ago, the typical literary gent wrote books on baroque architecture and had a soul above politics. But that attitude is becoming difficult and even unfashionable. The times are growing harsher, the issues are clearer, the belief that nothing will ever change (i.e. that your dividends will always be safe) is less prevalent. The fence on which the literary gent sits, once as comfortable as the plush cushion of a cathedral stall, is now pinching his bottom intolerably; more and more he shows a disposition to drop off on one side or the other. It is interesting to notice how many of our leading writers, who a dozen years ago were art for art's saking for all they were worth and would have considered it too vulgar for words even to vote at a general election, are now taking a definite political standpoint; while most of the younger writers, at least those of them who are not mere footlers, have been " political " from the start. I believe that when the pinch comes there is a terrible danger that the main movement of the intelligentsia will be towards Fascism. Just how soon the pinch will come it is difficult to say; it depends, probably, upon events in Europe; but it may be that within two years or even a year we shall have reached the decisive moment. That will also be the moment when every person with any brains or any decency will know in his bones that he ought to be on the Socialist side.

But he will not necessarily come there of his own accord; there are too many ancient prejudices standing in the way. He will have to be persuaded, and by methods that imply an understanding of his viewpoint. Socialists cannot afford to waste any more time in preaching to the converted. Their job now is to make Socialists as rapidly as possible; instead of which, all too often, they are making Fascists.

When I speak of Fascism in England, I am not necessarily thinking of Mosley and his pimpled followers. English Fascism, when it arrives, is likely to be of a sedate and subtle kind (presumably, at any rate at first, it won't be *called* Fascism), and it is doubtful whether a Gilbert and Sullivan heavy dragoon of Mosley's stamp would ever be much more than a joke to the majority of English people; though even Mosley will bear watching, for experience shows (*vide* the careers of Hitler, Napoleon III) that to a political climber it is sometimes an advantage not to be taken too seriously at the beginning of his career. But what I am thinking of at this moment is the Fascist attitude of mind, which beyond any doubt is gaining ground among people who ought to know better. Fascism as it appears in the intellectual is a sort of mirror-image—not actually of Socialism but of a plausible travesty of Socialism. It boils down to a determination to do the *opposite* of whatever the mythical Socialist does. If you present Socialism in a bad and misleading light—if you let people imagine that it does not mean much more than pouring European civilisation down the sink at the command of Marxist prigs—you risk driving the intellectual into Fascism. You frighten him into a sort of angry defensive attitude in which he simply refuses to listen to the Socialist case. Some such attitude is already quite clearly discernible in writers like Pound, Wyndham Lewis, Roy Campbell, etc., in most of the Roman Catholic writers and many of the Douglas Credit group, in certain popular novelists and even, if one looks below the surface, in su-superior conservative highbrows like Eliot and his countless followers. If you want some unmistakable illustrations of the growth of Fascist feeling in England, have a look at some of the innumerable letters that were written to the Press during the Abyssinian war, approving the Italian action, and also the howl of glee that went up from both Catholic and Anglican pulpits (see the *Daily Mail* of August 17th, 1936) over the Fascist rising in Spain.

In order to combat Fascism it is necessary to understand it, which involves admitting that it contains some good as well as much evil. In practice, of course, it is merely an infamous tyranny, and its methods of attaining and holding power are such that even its most ardent apologists prefer to talk about something else. But the underlying feeling of Fascism, the feeling that first draws people into the Fascist camp, may be less contemptible. It is not *always*, as the *Saturday Review* would lead one to suppose, a squealing terror of the Bolshevik bogey-man. Everyone who has given the movement so much as a glance knows that the rank-and-file Fascist is often quite a well-meaning person—quite genuinely anxious, for instance, to better the lot of the unemployed. But more important than this is the fact that Fascism draws its strength from the good as well as the bad varieties of conservatism. To anyone with a feeling for tradition and for discipline it comes with its appeal ready-made. Probably it is very easy, when you have had a bellyful of the more tactless kind of Socialist propaganda, to see Fascism as the last line defence of

all that is good in European civilisation. Even the
Fascist bully at his symbolic worst, with rubber truncheon
in one hand and castor oil bottle in the other, does not
necessarily feel himself a bully; more probably he feels
like Roland in the pass at Roncevaux, defending
Christendom against the barbarian. We have got to
admit that if Fascism is everywhere advancing, this is
largely the fault of Socialists themselves. Partly it is
due to the mistaken Communist tactic of sabotaging
democracy, i.e. sawing off the branch you are sitting on;
but still more to the fact that Socialists have, so to speak,
presented their case wrong side foremost. They have
never made it sufficiently clear that the essential aims
of Socialism are justice and liberty. With their eyes
glued to economic facts, they have proceeded on the
assumption that man has no soul, and explicitly or
implicitly they have set up the goal of a materialistic
Utopia. As a result Fascism has been able to play upon
every instinct that revolts against hedonism and a cheap
conception of " progress." It has been able to pose as
the upholder of the European tradition, and to appeal
to Christian belief, to patriotism and to the military
virtues. It is far worse than useless to write Fascism
off as " mass sadism," or some easy phrase of that kind.
If you pretend that it is merely an aberration which will
presently pass off of its own accord, you are dreaming
a dream from which you will awake when somebody
coshes you with a rubber truncheon. The only possible
course is to examine the Fascist case, grasp that there is
something to be said for it, and then make it clear to
the world that whatever good Fascism contains is also
implicit in Socialism.

   At present the situation is desperate. Even if nothing
worse befalls us, there are the conditions which I

described in the earlier part of this book and which
are not going to improve under our present economic
system. Still more urgent is the danger of Fascist domi-
nation in Europe. And unless Socialist doctrine, in an
effective form, can be diffused widely and very quickly,
there is no certainty that Fascism will ever be overthrown. For Socialism is the only real enemy that
Fascism has to face. The capitalist-imperialist govern-
ments, even though they themselves are about to be
plundered, will not fight with any conviction against
Fascism as such. Our rulers, those of them who understand the issue, would probably prefer to hand over
every square inch of the British Empire to Italy,
Germany and Japan than to see Socialism triumphant.
It was easy to laugh at Fascism when we imagined that
it was based on hysterical nationalism, because it seemed
obvious that the Fascist states, each regarding itself
as the chosen people and patriotic *contra mundum*,
would clash with one another. But nothing of the kind
is happening. Fascism is now an international movement, which means not only that the Fascist nations
can combine for purposes of loot, but that they are
groping, perhaps only half consciously as yet, towards
a world-system. For the vision of the totalitarian state
there is being substituted the vision of the totalitarian
world. As I pointed out earlier, the advance of machine-
technique must lead ultimately to some form of collectivism, but that form need not necessarily be equalitarian;
that is, it need not be Socialism. *Pace* the economists,
it is quite easy to imagine a world-society, economically
collectivist—that is, with the profit principle eliminated
—but with all political, military and educational
power in the hands of a small caste of rulers and their
bravos. That or something like it is the objective of

Fascism. And that, of course, is the slave-state, or rather the slave-world; it would probably be a stable form of society, and the chances are, considering the enormous wealth of the world if scientifically exploited, that the slaves would be well-fed and contented. It is usual to speak of the Fascist objective as the " beehive state," which does a grave injustice to bees. A world of rabbits ruled by stoats would be nearer the mark. It is against this beastly possibility that we have got to combine.

The only thing *for* which we can combine is the underlying ideal of Socialism; justice and liberty. But it is hardly strong enough to call this ideal " underlying." It is almost completely forgotten. It has been buried beneath layer after layer of doctrinaire priggishness, party squabbles and half-baked " progressivism " until it is like a diamond hidden under a mountain of dung. The job of the Socialist is to get it out again. Justice and liberty ! *Those* are the words that have got to ring like a bugle across the world. For a long time past, certainly for the last ten years, the devil has had all the best tunes. We have reached a stage when the very word " Socialism " calls up, on the one hand, a picture of aeroplanes, tractors and huge glittering factories of glass and concrete; on the other, a picture of vegetarians with wilting beards, of Bolshevik commissars (half gangster, half gramophone), of earnest ladies in sandals, shock-headed Marxists chewing polysyllables, escaped Quakers, birth-control fanatics and Labour Party backstairs-crawlers. Socialism, at least in this island, does not smell any longer of revolution and the overthrow of tyrants; it smells of crankishness, machine-worship and the stupid cult of Russia. Unless you can remove that smell, and very rapidly, Fascism may win.

CHAPTER XIII

AND FINALLY, is there anything one can do about it?

In the first part of this book I illustrated, by a few brief sidelights, the kind of mess we are in; in this second part I have been trying to explain why, in my opinion, so many normal decent people are repelled by the only remedy, namely by Socialism. Obviously the most urgent need of the next few years is to capture those normal decent ones before Fascism plays its trump card. I do not want to raise here the question of parties and political expedients. More important than any party label (though doubtless the mere menace of Fascism will presently bring some kind of Popular Front into existence) is the diffusion of Socialist doctrine in an effective form. People have got to be made ready to *act* as Socialists. There are, I believe, countless people who, without being aware of it, are in sympathy with the essential aims of Socialism, and who could be won over almost without a struggle if only one could find the word that would move them. Everyone who knows the meaning of poverty, everyone who has a genuine hatred of tyranny and war, is on the Socialist side, potentially. My job here, therefore, is to suggest—necessarily in very general terms—how a reconciliation might be effected between Socialism and its more intelligent enemies.

First, as to the enemies themselves—I mean all those people who grasp that capitalism is evil but who are

conscious of a sort of queasy, shuddering sensation when
Socialism is mentioned. As I have pointed out, this is
traceable to two main causes. One is the personal
inferiority of many individual Socialists; the other is
the fact that Socialism is too often coupled with a fat-
bellied, godless conception of " progress " which revolts
anyone with a feeling for tradition or the rudiments of
an æsthetic sense. Let me take the second point first.

The distaste for " progress " and machine-civilisation
which is so common among sensitive people is only
defensible as an attitude of mind. It is not valid as a
reason for rejecting Socialism, because it presupposes an
alternative which does not exist. When you say, " I
object to mechanisation and standardisation—therefore
I object to Socialism," you are saying in effect, " I am
free to do without the machine if I choose," which is
nonsense. We are all dependent upon the machine, and
if the machines stopped working most of us would die.
You may hate the machine-civilisation, probably you
are right to hate it, but for the present there can be no
question of accepting or rejecting it. The machine-
civilisation *is here*, and it can only be criticised from the
inside, because all of us are inside it. It is only romantic
fools who flatter themselves that they have escaped, like
the literary gent in his Tudor cottage with bathroom
h. and c., and the he-man who goes off to live a " primitive " life in the jungle with a Mannlicher rifle and four
wagon-loads of tinned food. And almost certainly the
machine-civilisation will continue to triumph. There is
no reason to think that it will destroy itself or stop func-
tioning of its own accord. For some time past it has been
fashionable to say that war is presently going to " wreck
civilisation " altogether; but, though the next full-sized
war will certainly be horrible enough to make all

previous ones seem a joke, it is immensely unlikely that it will put a stop to mechanical progress. It is true that a very vulnerable country like England, and perhaps the whole of western Europe, could be reduced to chaos by a few thousand well-placed bombs, but no war is at present thinkable which could wipe out industrialism in all countries simultaneously. We may take it that the return to a simpler, freer, less mechanised way of life, however desirable it may be, is not going to happen. This is not fatalism, it is merely acceptance of facts. It is meaningless to oppose Socialism on the ground that you object to the beehive State, for the beehive State *is here*. The choice is not, as yet, between a human and an inhuman world. It is simply between Socialism and Fascism, which at its very best is Socialism with the virtues left out.

The job of the thinking person, therefore, is not to reject Socialism but to make up his mind to humanise it. Once Socialism is in a way to being established, those who can see through the swindle of " progress " will probably find themselves resisting. In fact, it is their special function to do so. In the machine-world they have got to be a sort of permanent opposition, which is not the same thing as being an obstructionist or a traitor. But in this I am speaking of the future. For the moment the only possible course for any decent person, however much of a Tory or an anarchist by temperament, is to work for the establishment of Socialism. Nothing else can save us from the misery of the present or the nightmare of the future. To oppose Socialism *now*, when twenty million Englishmen are underfed and Fascism has conquered half Europe, is suicidal. It is like starting a civil war when the Goths are crossing the frontier.

Therefore it is all the more important to get rid of

that mere nervous prejudice against Socialism which is not founded on any serious objection. As I have pointed out already, many people who are not repelled by Socialism are repelled by Socialists. Socialism, as now presented, is unattractive largely because it appears, at any rate from the outside, to be the plaything of cranks, doctrinaires, parlour Bolsheviks and so forth. But it is worth remembering that this is only so because the cranks, doctrinaires, etc., have been allowed to get there first; if the movement were invaded by better brains and more common decency, the objectionable types would cease to dominate it. For the present one must just set one's teeth and ignore them; they will loom much smaller when the movement has been humanised. Besides, they are irrelevant. We have got to fight for justice and liberty, and Socialism does mean justice and liberty when the nonsense is stripped off it. It is only the essentials that are worth remembering. To recoil from Socialism because so many individual Socialists are inferior people is as absurd as refusing to travel by train because you dislike the ticket-collector's face.

And secondly, as to the Socialist himself—more especially the vocal, tract-writing type of Socialist.

We are at a moment when it is desperately necessary for left-wingers of all complexions to drop their differences and hang together. Indeed this is already happening to a small extent. Obviously, then, the more intransigent kind of Socialist has now got to ally himself with people who are not in perfect agreement with him. As a rule he is rightly unwilling to do so, because he sees the very real danger of watering the whole Socialist movement down to some kind of pale-pink humbug even more ineffectual than the parliamentary Labour

Party. At the moment, for instance, there is great danger that the Popular Front which Fascism will presumably bring into existence will not be genuinely Socialist in character, but will simply be a manœuvre against German and Italian (not English) Fascism. Thus the need to unite against Fascism might draw the Socialist into alliance with his very worst enemies. But the principle to go upon is this: that you are never in danger of allying yourself with the wrong people provided that you keep the essentials of your movement in the foreground. And what are the essentials of Socialism? What is the mark of a real Socialist? I suggest that the real Socialist is one who wishes—not merely conceives it as desirable, but actively wishes—to see tyranny overthrown. But I fancy that the majority of orthodox Marxists would not accept that definition, or would only accept it very grudgingly. Sometimes, when I listen to these people talking, and still more when I read their books, I get the impression that, to them, the whole Socialist movement is no more than a kind of exciting heresy-hunt—a leaping to and fro of frenzied witch-doctors to the beat of tom-toms and the tune of " Fee, fi, fo, fum, I smell the blood of a right-wing deviationist!" It is because of this kind of thing that it is so much easier to feel yourself a Socialist when you are among working-class people. The working-class Socialist, like the working-class Catholic, is weak on doctrine and can hardly open his mouth without uttering a heresy, but he has the heart of the matter in him. He does grasp the central fact that Socialism means the overthrow of tyranny, and the " Marseillaise," if it were translated for his benefit, would appeal to him more deeply than any learned treatise on dialectical materialism. At this moment it is waste of time to insist that acceptance of Socialism means acceptance of the philosophic side of Marxism, plus adulation of Russia. The Socialist movement has not time to be a league of dialectical materialists; it has got to be a league of the oppressed against the oppressors. You have got to attract the man who means business, and you have got to drive away the mealy-mouthed Liberal who wants foreign Fascism destroyed in order that he may go on drawing his dividends peacefully—the type of humbug who passes resolutions " against Fascism and Communism," i.e. against rats and rat-poison. Socialism means the overthrow of tyranny, at home as well as abroad. So long as you keep *that* fact well to the front, you will never be in much doubt as to who are your real supporters. As for minor differences—and the profoundest philosophical difference is unimportant compared with saving the twenty million Englishmen whose bones are rotting from malnutrition—the time to argue about them is afterwards.

I do not think the Socialist need make any sacrifice of essentials, but certainly he will have to make a great sacrifice of externals. It would help enormously, for instance, if the smell of crankishness which still clings to the Socialist movement could be dispelled. If only the sandals and the pistachio-coloured shirts could be put in a pile and burnt, and every vegetarian, teetotaller and creeping Jesus sent home to Welwyn Garden City to do his yoga exercises quietly ! But that, I am afraid, is not going to happen. What *is* possible, however, is for the more intelligent kind of Socialist to stop alienating possible supporters in silly and quite irrelevant ways. There are so many minor priggishnesses which could so easily be dropped. Take for instance the dreary attitude of the typical Marxist towards literature. Out of the many that come into my mind, I will give just one example. It sounds trivial, but it isn't. In the old *Worker's Weekly* (one of the forerunners of the *Daily Worker*) there used to be a column of literary chat of the "Books on the Editor's Table" type. For several weeks running there had been a certain amount of talk about Shakespeare; whereupon an incensed reader wrote to say, "Dear Comrade, we don't want to hear about these bourgeois writers like Shakespeare. Can't you give us something a bit more proletarian?" etc., etc. The editor's reply was simple. "If you will turn to the index of Marx's *Capital*," he wrote, "you will find that Shakespeare is mentioned several times." And please notice that this was enough to silence the objector. Once Shakespeare had received the benediction of Marx, he became respectable. *That* is the mentality that drives ordinary sensible people away from the Socialist movement. You do not need to care about Shakespeare to be repelled by that kind of thing. Again, there is the horrible jargon that nearly all Socialists think it necessary to employ. When the ordinary person hears phrases like "bourgeois ideology" and "proletarian solidarity" and "expropriation of the expropriators," he is not inspired by them, he is merely disgusted. Even the single word "Comrade" has done its dirty little bit towards discrediting the Socialist movement. How many a waverer has halted on the brink, gone perhaps to some public meeting and watched self-conscious Socialists dutifully addressing one another as "Comrade," and then slid away, disillusioned, into the nearest four-ale bar! And his instinct is sound; for where is the sense of sticking on to yourself a ridiculous label which even after long practice can hardly be mentioned without a gulp of shame? It is fatal to let the ordinary enquirer get away with the idea that being a Socialist means wearing sandals and burbling about dialectical materialism. You have got to make it clear that there is room in the Socialist movement for human beings, or the game is up.

And this raises a great difficulty. It means that the issue of class, as distinct from mere economic status, has got to be faced more realistically than it is being faced at present.

I devoted three chapters to discussing the class-difficulty. The principal fact that will have emerged, I think, is that though the English class-system has out-lived its usefulness, it *has* outlived it and shows no signs of dying. It greatly confuses the issue to assume, as the orthodox Marxist so often does (see for instance Mr. Alec Brown's in some ways interesting book, *The Fate of the Middle Classes*), that social status is determined solely by income. Economically, no doubt, there are only two classes, the rich and the poor, but socially there is a whole hierarchy of classes, and the manners and traditions learned by each class in childhood are not only very different but—this is the essential point—generally persist from birth to death. Hence the anomalous individuals that you find in every class of society. You find writers like Wells and Bennett who have grown immensely rich and have yet preserved intact their lower-middle-class Nonconformist pre-judices; you find millionaires who cannot pronounce their aitches; you find petty shopkeepers whose income is far lower than that of the bricklayer and who, never-theless, consider themselves (and are considered) the bricklayer's social superiors; you find board-school boys ruling Indian provinces and public-school men touting vacuum cleaners. If social stratification corresponded precisely to economic stratification, the public-school man would assume a cockney accent the day his income dropped below £200 a year. But does he? On the contrary, he immediately becomes twenty times more Public School than before. He clings to the Old School Tie as to a life-line. And even the aitchless millionaire, though sometimes he goes to an elocutionist and learns a B.B.C. accent, seldom succeeds in disguising himself as completely as he would like to. It is in fact very difficult to escape, culturally, from the class into which you have been born.

As prosperity declines, social anomalies grow commoner. You don't get more aitchless millionaires, but you do get more and more public-school men touting vacuum cleaners and more and more small shopkeepers driven into the workhouse. Large sections of the middle class are being gradually proletarianised; but the important point is that they do not, at any rate in the first generation, adopt a proletarian outlook. Here am I, for instance, with a bourgeois upbringing and a working-class income. Which class do I belong to? Economically I belong to the working class, but it is almost impossible for me to think of myself as anything but a member of the bourgeoisie. And supposing I had to take sides, whom should I side with, the upper class which is trying to squeeze me out of existence, or the working class whose manners are not my manners? It is probable that I personally, in any important issue, would side with the working class. But what about the tens or hundreds of thousands of others who are in approximately the same position? And what about that far larger class, running into millions this time—the office-workers and black-coated employees of all kinds—whose traditions are less definitely middle class but who would

certainly not thank you if you called them proletarians?
All of these people have the same interests and the same
enemies as the working class. All are being robbed and
bullied by the same system. Yet how many of them
realise it? When the pinch came nearly all of them
would side with their oppressors and against those who
ought to be their allies. It is quite easy to imagine a
middle class crushed down to the worst depths of poverty
and still remaining bitterly anti-working class in sentiment; this being, of course, a ready-made Fascist Party.

Obviously the Socialist movement has got to capture
the exploited middle class before it is too late; above all
it must capture the office-workers, who are so numerous
and, if they knew how to combine, so powerful. Equally
obviously it has so far failed to do so. The very last
person in whom you can hope to find revolutionary
opinions is a clerk or a commercial traveller. Why?
Very largely, I think, because of the " proletarian "
cant with which Socialist propaganda is mixed up. In
order to symbolise the class war, there has been set up
the more or less mythical figure of a " proletarian," a
muscular but downtrodden man in greasy overalls, in
contradistinction to a " capitalist," a fat, wicked man
in a top hat and fur coat. It is tacitly assumed that there
is no one in between; the truth being, of course, that in
a country like England about a quarter of the population is in between. If you are going to harp on the
" dictatorship of the proletariat," it is an elementary
precaution to start by explaining who the proletariat
are. But because of the Socialist tendency to idealise the
manual worker as such, this has never been made
sufficiently clear. How many of the wretched shivering
army of clerks and shopwalkers, who in some ways are
actually worse off than a miner or a dock-hand, think of

themselves as proletarians? A proletarian—so they have been taught to think—means a man without a collar. So that when you try to move them by talking about "class war," you only succeed in scaring them; they forget their incomes and remember their accents, and fly to the defence of the class that is exploiting them.

Socialists have a big job ahead of them here. They have got to demonstrate, beyond possibility of doubt, just where the line of cleavage between exploiter and exploited comes. Once again it is a question of sticking to essentials; and the essential point here is that all people with small, insecure incomes are in the same boat and ought to be fighting on the same side. Probably we could do with a little less talk about "capitalist" and "proletarian" and a little more about the robbers and the robbed. But at any rate we must drop that misleading habit of pretending that the only proletarians are manual labourers. It has got to be brought home to the clerk, the engineer, the commercial traveller, the middle-class man who has "come down in the world," the village grocer, the lower-grade civil servant and all other doubtful cases that they *are* the proletariat, and that Socialism means a fair deal for them as well as for the navvy and the factory-hand. They must not be allowed to think that the battle is between those who pronounce their aitches and those who don't; for if they think that, they will join in on the side of the aitches.

I am implying that different classes must be persuaded to act together without, for the moment, being asked to drop their class-differences. And that sounds dangerous. It sounds rather too like the Duke of York's summer camp and that dismal line of talk about class-co-operation and putting our shoulders to the wheel, which is

eyewash or Fascism, or both. There can be no co-operation between classes whose real interests are opposed.
The capitalist cannot co-operate with the proletarian.
The cat cannot co-operate with the mouse; and if the
cat does suggest co-operation and the mouse is fool
enough to agree, in a very little while the mouse will be
disappearing down the cat's throat. But it is always
possible to co-operate so long as it is upon a basis of
common interests. The people who have got to act
together are all those who cringe to the boss and all
those who shudder when they think of the rent. This
means that the small-holder has got to ally himself with
the factory-hand, the typist with the coal-miner, the
schoolmaster with the garage mechanic. There is some
hope of getting them to do so if they can be made to
understand where their interest lies. But this will not
happen if their social prejudices, which in some of them
are at least as strong as any economic consideration,
are needlessly irritated. There is, after all, a real difference of manners and traditions between a bank clerk
and a dock labourer, and the bank clerk's feeling of
superiority is very deeply rooted. Later on he will have
to get rid of it, but this is not a good moment for asking
him to do so. Therefore it would be a very great advantage if that rather meaningless and mechanical bourgeois-
baiting, which is a part of nearly all Socialist propaganda,
could be dropped for the time being. Throughout left-
wing thought and writing—and the whole way through
it, from the leading articles in the *Daily Worker* to the
comic columns in the *News Chronicle*—there runs an
anti-genteel tradition, a persistent and often very stupid
gibing at genteel mannerisms and genteel loyalties (or,
in Communist jargon, " bourgeois values.") It is largely
humbug, coming as it does from bourgeois-baiters who

are bourgeois themselves, but it does great harm, because it allows a minor issue to block a major one. It directs attention away from the central fact that poverty is poverty, whether the tool you work with is a pick-axe or a fountain pen.

Once again, here am I, with my middle-class origins and my income of about three pounds a week from all sources. For what I am worth it would be better to get me in on the Socialist side than to turn me into a Fascist. But if you are constantly bullying me about my " bourgeois ideology," if you give me to understand that in some subtle way I am an inferior person because I have never worked with my hands, you will only succeed in antagonising me. For you are telling me either that I am inherently useless or that I ought to alter myself in some way that is beyond my power. I cannot proletarianise my accent or certain of my tastes and beliefs, and I would not if I could. Why should I? I don't ask anybody else to speak my dialect; why should anybody else ask me to speak his? It would be far better to take these miserable class-stigmata for granted and emphasise them as little as possible. They are comparable to a race-difference, and experience shows that one *can* co-operate with foreigners, even with foreigners whom one dislikes, when it is really necessary. Economically, I am in the same boat with the miner, the navvy and the farm-hand; remind me of that and I will fight at their side. But culturally I am different from the miner, the navvy and the farm-hand; lay the emphasis on that and you may arm me against them. If I were a solitary anomaly I should not matter, but what is true of myself is true of countless others. Every bank clerk dreaming of the sack, every shopkeeper teetering on the brink of bankruptcy, is in essentially the same position. These are the sinking middle class, and most of them are clinging to their gentility under the impression that it keeps them afloat. It is not good policy to *start* by telling them to throw away the life-belt. There is a quite obvious danger that in the next few years large sections of the middle class will make a sudden and violent swing to the Right. In doing so they may become formidable. The weakness of the middle class hitherto has lain in the fact that they have never learned to combine; but if you frighten them into combining *against* you, you may find that you have raised up a devil. We had a brief glimpse of this possibility in the General Strike.

To sum up: There is no chance of righting the conditions I described in the earlier chapters of this book, or of saving England from Fascism, unless we can bring an effective Socialist party into existence. It will have to be a party with genuinely revolutionary intentions, and it will have to be numerically strong enough to act. We can only get it if we offer an objective which fairly ordinary people will recognise as desirable. Beyond all else, therefore, we need intelligent propaganda. Less about " class consciousness," " expropriation of the expropriators," " bourgeois ideology," and " proletarian solidarity," not to mention the sacred sisters, thesis, antithesis and synthesis; and more about justice, liberty and the plight of the unemployed. And less about mechanical progress, tractors, the Dneiper dam and the latest salmon-canning factory in Moscow; that kind of thing is not an integral part of Socialist doctrine, and it drives away many people whom the Socialist cause needs, including most of those who can hold a pen. All that is needed is to hammer two facts home into the public consciousness. One, that the interests of all exploited people are the same;

the other, that Socialism is compatible with common decency.

As for the terribly difficult issue of class-distinctions, the only possible policy for the moment is to go easy and not frighten more people than can be helped. And above all, no more of those muscular-curate efforts at class-breaking. If you belong to the bourgeoisie, don't be too eager to bound forward and embrace your proletarian brothers; they may not like it, and if they show that they don't like it you will probably find that your class-prejudices are not so dead as you imagined. And if you belong to the proletariat, by birth or in the sight of God, don't sneer too automatically at the Old School Tie; it covers loyalties which can be useful to you if you know how to handle them.

Yet I believe there is some hope that when Socialism is a living issue, a thing that large numbers of Englishmen genuinely care about, the class-difficulty may solve itself more rapidly than now seems thinkable. In the next few years we shall either get that effective Socialist party that we need, or we shall not get it. If we do not get it, then Fascism is coming; probably a slimy Anglicised form of Fascism, with cultured policemen instead of Nazi gorillas and the lion and the unicorn instead of the swastika. But if we do get it there will be a struggle, conceivably a physical one, for our plutocracy will not sit quiet under a genuinely revolutionary government. And when the widely separate classes who, necessarily, would form any real Socialist party have fought side by side, they may feel differently about one another. And then perhaps this misery of class-prejudice will fade away, and we of the sinking middle class—the private schoolmaster, the half-starved free-lance journalist, the colonel's spinster daughter with £75 a year, the jobless

Cambridge graduate, the ship's officer without a ship, the clerks, the civil servants, the commercial travellers and the thrice-bankrupt drapers in the country towns— may sink without further struggles into the working class where we belong, and probably when we get there it will not be so dreadful as we feared, for, after all, we have nothing to lose but our aitches.

THE END

Books by George Orwell
available from Harcourt, Inc.
in Harvest paperback editions

BURMESE DAYS

A CLERGYMAN'S DAUGHTER

A COLLECTION OF ESSAYS

COMING UP FOR AIR

DICKENS, DALI & OTHERS

DOWN AND OUT IN PARIS AND LONDON

HOMAGE TO CATALONIA

IN FRONT OF YOUR NOSE: THE COLLECTED ESSAYS,
JOURNALISM, AND LETTERS OF GEORGE ORWELL, 1945–1950

KEEP THE ASPIDISTRA FLYING

THE ORWELL READER:
FICTION, ESSAYS AND REPORTAGE

THE ROAD TO WIGAN PIER